NINETEENTH-CENTURY SUSPENSE

Nineteenth-Century Suspense

From Poe to Conan Doyle

Edited by
Clive Bloom, Brian Docherty, Jane Gibb
and Keith Shand

St. Martin's Press   New York

© 1988

First published in the United States of America in 1988

Printed in Great Britain

ISBN 0–312–01677–8

Library of Congress Cataloging-in-Publication Data
Nineteenth-century suspense.
Bibliography: p.
Includes index.
1. Detectives and mystery stories, English—History
and criticism.   2. Detective and mystery stories,
American—History and criticism.   3. English fiction,
19th century—History and criticism.   4. American
fiction—19th century—History and criticism.   I. Bloom,
Clive.   II. Title: 19th-century suspense.
PR868.D4N56   1988   823'.0872'08   87–33631
ISBN 0–312–01677–8

Contents

Preface

This volume presents nine concise essays by literary authorities. Each essay combines, in a clear and understandable way, contemporary literary theory and sound practical criticism. Articles cover Edgar Allan Poe, Arthur Conan Doyle, Bram Stoker, Charles Dickens, Robert Louis Stevenson, the detective genre, the ghost story and arguments about the emergence and importance of detective fiction, the conditions governing the relationship between sexuality and meaning in *Dracula*, and concepts of colonialism and evolution. This volume comprehensively covers and combines contemporary debates over post-structuralism, the politics of the body and notions of gender with formal questions about genre and its social significance. The volume finishes with a consideration of the significance of Jack the Ripper and real murder in the nineteenth century.

Acknowledgements

Thanks are due to David Green for all his help and advice, to Graham Greenglass for his artistic guidance, to Frances and Leon Kacher for their invaluable assistance, and to Ilana Scott and Lesley Bloom for patiently typing the manuscript. Special thanks are also due to Frances Arnold, to Graham Eyre and to Mary Shakeshaft, whose careful work helped the project reach completion.

Notes on the Contributors

Clive Bloom is Lecturer in English at Middlesex Polytechnic. He is author of *The 'Occult' Experience and the New Criticism*, and has just completed a book on Edgar Allan Poe and Sigmund Freud.

Anne Cranny-Francis lectures in the Faculty of Humanities and Social Sciences at the New South Wales Institute of Technology, Sydney, Australia. She is an authority on Victorian and Australian literature, and is preparing a study on Christina Stead.

Howard Davies is Senior Lecturer at the Polytechnic of North London and has numerous published articles on French literature. At present he is preparing a history of *Les Temps modernes*.

Gary Day teaches English and Drama in Brighton, and is a contributor to *The Dickensian*.

Philip Martin is Lecturer at King Alfred's College, Winchester, and is the author of *Mad Women in Romantic Literature*.

David Punter is Lecturer in English and American studies at the University of East Anglia and is the author of numerous articles and books, including *The Literature of Terror*.

Nick Rance is Lecturer in English at Middlesex Polytechnic and is the author of *The Historical Novel and Popular Politics in Nineteenth-Century England*. He is now preparing a book on Wilkie Collins.

1

Edgar Allan Poe: Tales of Dark Heat

DAVID PUNTER

Reading through Poe's tales is a peculiar experience. In some ways, of course, they can be readily seen to be by the same hand. There are continuing and, indeed, at times irritatingly repetitive preoccupations, ranging from, for instance, fear of premature burial at the 'Gothic' end of the scale to a fascination with specific technological developments – the balloon, mesmerism, various kinds of medical progress. There are also similarities of form caused largely by the actual circumstances of the production of the stories: it is not entirely a joke, for instance, when Poe asserts in 'How to Write a Blackwood Article' that no story can be published in *Blackwood's* unless it contains at least one erudite quotation from the classics, even if on occasion it is not entirely to the point.[1]

And yet it is significant differences which attract the attention. Across the whole corpus, there are only a few tales which seem to muster the writer's entire concentration. They are often the shortest; they are often marked out by not beginning with the 'naturalising' preambles of which Poe was so fond. They are, by and large, the tales which are well-known: pre-eminently, perhaps, 'The Cask of Amontillado', 'The Fall of the House of Usher', 'The Masque of the Red Death', 'The Pit and the Pendulum', 'Ligeia', 'The Tell-Tale Heart' and a few others – 'MS. Found in a Bottle', certainly, with its extraordinary image of the giant ship of death, and 'The Man of the Crowd', which still remains among the most significant images of urban alienation.

The oddest thing about this group of stories, and, in a way, the guarantee of their quality, is the remarkable sense of *déjà vu* which attends them. They are stories, of course, which have sunk deep into the cultural unconscious of the West; but it would be a one-sided judgement which left it at that without adding that, therefore, they must be reworkings of psychological materials

1

which were already foci of interest. And this cannot be divorced from a question of style: it is often in these stories that Poe moves directly into an incantatory mode which dissolves historical location and immediately encourages the reader to see them as parables of a continuous present rather than simply as accounts of past events. The stories are themselves – or appear to be – acts of rememoration, usually without a saving grace; these are events on which the mind cannot cease to play, and their only solution or resolution is death.

What I am describing, then, is a difference of intensity; it is only on rare occasions that Poe's full intensity is mustered. It is mustered in a different way in the 'detective' stories, such as 'The Murders in the Rue Morgue' and 'The Mystery of Marie Rogêt, whereas in the first group of stories it is in the service of a quite opposite psychic structure, which is dialectically related to the first. That is to say, there is an obvious connection between the emphasis on all-encompassing rational power, personated in Auguste Dupin – a power which itself, by a paradoxical process, comes to appear supernatural – and the fears of the dark, of entombment, of collapse and decay with which Poe's name has come to be mainly associated. The detective stories are predicated on an 'if only': if only the human reasoning capacity could indeed be made as strong as this, then our fears and terrors would disappear and we should be fully at home in a world which, alas, persists in presenting itself to us under the guise of mystery, the incomprehensible, the shiver of doubt.

'The Cask of Amontillado' is a particularly fascinating tale in this respect, because it unites, or attempts to unite, the universe of terror and the universe of order. Montresor's revenge, *outré* as it is, is none the less predicated on the basis of close and attentive planning. He has a distinct and amused eye for detail, on which he prides himself; there is an inseparability of madness and method, alluded to again in a more whimsical vein in 'The System of Dr Tarr and Prof. Fether', in which the lunatics actually do take over the asylum, although their winning attempts to build a substitute order are fraught with difficulty since at any moment one of them is likely to remember that, at heart, he is a frog or a teetotum. The most pleasing twist to 'Tarr and Fether' is that, when all is revealed and the lunatics show themselves in their true colours, there remains a puzzle about Maillard, the apparent director of the asylum. He, clearly, is a lunatic, and the one who has managed to impose his version of order on his fellow inmates; but he is also, it transpires, the real Maillard, who was indeed the director of the asylum until he lost his wits and was himself incarcerated. The result of his incarceration was that he formed the opinion that he was, really, the best man to run the asylum; and at first glance it is not easy to say whether his conviction, insane or not, has been proved wrong.

Returning, however, to 'The Cask of Amontillado', we again find Poe overturning a world, but less in terms of the ever-ambiguous structure of madness than in terms of language. First, the whole story is an elaborate structure of puns.[2] There are, obviously, the names: 'Montresor' and 'Fortunato'. There is the moment when, already within the damp cellars, Fortunato coughs and Montresor feigns solicitude for his health. 'I shall not', observes Fortunato, 'die of a cough.' 'True – true', responds Montresor. There is the visual pun of the arms of the Montresor family: 'a huge human foot d'or, in a field azure; the foot crushes a serpent rampant whose fangs are imbedded in the heel'. 'And the motto?' inquires Fortunato; *'Nemo me impune lacessit'*, comes the reply. To classify this as a pun, of course, is to call upon the theory of the joke which has developed from Freud; very briefly stated, a joke can only occur as a socio-linguistic interplay involving three positions: the teller of the joke, the hearer who understands, and the hearer who does not understand. Not all of these three positions need to be occupied at the level of the Real; but unless there is, at least implicitly, a duality of reception postures there is no psychic release, no laughter – and, of course, no reinforcement of the bond thus formed between teller and understanding hearer, a bond which may in fact be the principal social effect of jokes. Here, of course, Montresor and the reader (and, at a different level of narrative structure, the narrator and the reader) are bonded against Fortunato; although this does not, of course, preclude the psychic countermove by means of which we rebel at the position of conspirator in which we thus find ourselves.

Behind the puns – and the most elaborate is the play on 'masonry' which continues throughout, as brotherhood but simul-taneously as the culmination of murderous vengeance – lies something else. Fortunato's death is offered to us in the guise of a progressive relocation of meaning. At the beginning of the tale he is drunk, and thus not well equipped to follow the intricacies of Montresor's word-play. He is duped, certainly, into a belief in a false version of power: it is intrinsic to Montresor's plan that Fortunato must be the one eager to visit the vaults, and thus that, at the linguistic level, the desire is clothed in the victim's words and not in Montresor's. Fortunato's cough prefigures his descent into speechlessness, as does his apparent inability to derive meaning from the Latin motto.

In this context, the moment when Fortunato makes a masonic ritual gesture figures as an attempt to fight back, to impose a meaning on Montresor; but Montresor counters by producing a trowel, thus simultaneously regaining semiotic power and relegating Fortunato's universe of discourse to the ineffectually symbolic. Behind all this, there is also the shifting meaning of the word 'Amontillado' which Fortunato can only interpret literally, whereas Montresor is deliberately converting it into an imitation 'shifter'. When Fortunato is first chained within the recess which will become his tomb, for instance: ' "The Amontillado!" ejaculated my friend, not yet recovered from his astonishment.' 'True,' replies Montresor, 'the Amontillado'; but by this time it has become clear that the Amontillado stands, for Montresor, for the consummation of his desire, his vengeance decked out in a quite different sign of which he and he alone is the custodian. It is after this point that Fortunato is reduced to non-linguistic communication – a 'low moaning cry', followed by 'furious vibrations of the chain', and then 'a succession of loud and shrill screams'.

When these prove of no avail, Fortunato's final resort is to attempt to unravel the linguistic trickery which has been the means of his downfall: it is, he asserts, all a joke, and in this he is absolutely right. But the joke is a structure of power, and this is finally reinforced in the last exchange between the two men, when Fortunato screams, 'For the love of God, Montresor', to which Montresor replies by merely repeating his words, while we, the readers, know that the meaning he is ascribing to them is quite different and, by this point, incontrovertible, since Fortunato's version of events, his narrative, is about to be silenced for ever. '*In pace requiescat!*', Montresor concludes his account, an account which has now attained the status of the true since his joke has taken on the material robes of power.

'Berenice' is perhaps a less well-known tale, but equally interesting in terms of the underlying psychological structure, and as a different version of the obsessional intensity which is worked through in 'The Cask of Amontillado'. In an almost hallucinatory way, it reminds the reader of 'Ligeia', 'Morella' and the other tales of female death and return, but with a very different *dénouement*. Egaeus is, as is again customary in these tales of Poe's, betrothed to his cousin, Berenice, and we are immediately told that Berenice is a victim of the also familiar wasting disease which appears to afflict most of Poe's heroines as the prospect of marriage comes closer.[3] But Egaeus is himself also sick, and in a way that Poe is at great pains to delineate carefully. It is a psychological morbidity; a 'morbid irritability of those properties of the mind in metaphysical science termed the *attentive*'. He clarifies this as follows:

> Yet let me not be misapprehended. – The undue, earnest, and morbid attention thus excited by objects in their own nature frivolous, must not be confounded in character with that ruminating propensity common to all mankind, and more especially indulged in by persons of ardent imagination.... In the one instance, the dreamer, or enthusiast, being interested by an object usually *not* frivolous, imperceptibly loses sight of this object in a wilderness of deductions and suggestions issuing therefrom, until, at the conclusion of a day dream *often replete with luxury*, he finds the *incitamentum* or first cause of his musings entirely vanished and forgotten. In my case the primary object was *invariably frivolous*, although assuming, through the medium of my distempered vision, a refracted and unreal importance. Few deductions, if any, were made; and those few pertinaciously returning in upon the original object as a centre. The meditations were *never* pleasurable; and, at the termination of the reverie, the first cause, so far from being out of sight, had attained that supernaturally exaggerated interest which was the prevailing feature of the disease.

There is an attempt here to distinguish between the productive intensity of the poet and the unproductive intensity of the neurotic; as a psychological description, it probably does not stand, but it remains a very important description of a desire on the part of the writer, and it thus serves as a key to the tales. The problem, clearly, is exorcism: once in the mind – and they may be said to be 'always already' in the mind – the kinds of fear which Poe writes about do not go away. Meditation makes them all the more intense; narrative structure is useless as a palliative, because there is *no way out* of the stories. Sexually, the condition is satyriasis: a permanent morbid excitement with no moment of relief. Epistemologically, it is a question of non-differentiation of object, a problem of arbitrary fixation.

Or is it? As the brief story unfolds, Berenice comes to Egaeus, near the point of her death:

> The forehead was high, and very pale, and singularly placid; and the once jetty hair fell partially over it, and overshadowed the hollow temples with innumerable ringlets now of a vivid yellow, and jarring discordantly, in their fantastic character, with the reigning melancholy of the countenance. The eyes were lifeless, and lustreless, and seemingly pupil-less, and I shrank involuntarily from their glassy stare to the contemplation of the thin and shrunken lips. They parted; and in a smile of peculiar meaning, *the teeth* of the changed Berenice disclosed themselves slowly to my view. Would to God that I had never beheld them, or that, having done so, I had died....

The rest of the story is predictable. Berenice dies and is buried. Egaeus goes into a trance, and when he is woken from it by a servant, his attention is called to various objects in his room: his clothes, 'muddy and clotted with gore'; a spade against the wall; a box on the table which 'slipped from my hands, and fell heavily, and burst into pieces; and from it, with a rattling sound, there rolled out some instruments of dental surgery, intermingled with thirty-two small, white and ivory-looking substances that were scattered to and fro about the floor'.

But this apparently arbitrary obsession is, of course, open to interpretation, of various kinds. The delusive smile which discloses terror is frequent in Poe; there is a variant on it in 'The Facts in the Case of M. Valdemar', when the dead man speaks but only with his (blackened) tongue; thus the words come from him but are not of him. There is also, lurking here, some echo of the psychoanalytic theory of the 'body in fragments';[4] Egaeus clearly finds it impossible to compose for himself an entire and integrated picture of his beloved (and that may itself have a root in the sexual problem of cousinhood). He cannot compose and hold a whole sign, so has to perform a practical synecdoche, taking a part to stand for the whole and to represent sureness against the inevitability of decay. It need not, of course, have been the teeth; but then if we return to the problem of satyriasis, of unslakable desire, then presumably the only solution would be the removal of the offending organ. Egaeus has taken steps, either to avoid castration by a displaced *vagina dentata*, or alternatively to reincorporate that parody of feminity within himself; yet it is significant that, at the end, he is unable to open the box, and it is only through the 'accident' of dropping it that the teeth are made to appear.[5]

I want to point to a connection between Poe's intensity and his use of the apparently arbitrary: it is as though, in most of the stories, it is necessary for him to set up a structure of probability, but this, oddly enough, has the effect of reducing narrative conviction. It is only in those stories in which he dispenses entirely with probability that we sense the urgency, the desperate sureness, which attends on indispensable unconscious functions. And thus the double bind: all the writer can be sure of is that which he cannot 'know', according to any model of consciousness. Either we follow Poe, rather tediously, through the mazes of an intelligent but contorted and sometimes ill-informed mind; or we accompany him with a savage simplicity to regions where the only evidence is the pressure of the narrative itself, and its replicatory undying quality.

'The Pit and the Pendulum', the best-known of Poe's stories, should therefore be a test case; and it is. We can, of course, analyse it in conventionally psychoanalytic terms. Briefly, this is a fable of the 'red room' – there are many others, one of the most important being H. G. Wells's story of that name, in which the identity of the fear which inhabits the haunted chamber is finally clarified as fear itself. And from the red room, and its increasing constriction, we are immediately in the territory of birth, of the womb, of primal fear. Nothing, our hero concludes at last, can prevent the increasing heat and decreasing size of his environment from forcing him down the pit; nothing can prevent his entry into the world of cold mortality. There is no alternative to being born; but neither is there anything more terrifying, because by being born one enters into the cycle of life and death, and one is forced out onto the dangerous road of mortality.

And yet, of course, this does not occur. There is a final paragraph:

There was a discordant hum of human voices! There was a loud blast as of many trumpets! There was a harsh grating as of a thousand thunders! The fiery walls rushed back! An outstretched arm caught my own as I fell, fainting, into the abyss. It was that of General Lasalle. The French army had entered Toledo. The Inquisition was in the hands of its enemies.

This is, of course, an extraordinary *dénouement*, largely in that it pretends to no connectedness whatever with the body of the tale. It is an absolute subversion of the idea of 'narrative development', the perfection of the *deus ex machina*. We can speculate a little more on its form: the central figure is saved by a character who is military; who represents secure strength; and who, uniquely in the story, is named. If we put these features together, we can produce a psychic peculiarity: that Poe, terrified in this case at the prospect of ejection into the world of death, experiences the 'name-of-the-Father', not as domination or oppression, but as salvation.[6] Lasalle is, of course, linguistically the 'room' under a different guise, the presumably more capacious room offered by masculinity, a masculinity which is armed and therefore sure of its power.

The hero of the story is thus rescued by an act of differentiation; his recognition of a named individual (unlikely, under the circumstances, as it might appear) is presumably a harbinger of the return of his own name, which has been in suspension. What is terrifying is *silence*: the silence which might be associated with premature burial, or, as in 'The Cask of Amontillado', with having one's version of events silenced; or, more importantly, that silence which betokens namelessness. Thus Poe's continual harping on the names – Berenice, Ligeia, Morella, Eleanora, and more so again in his poetry. Yet these names provide no escape, for they are, typically, the names of the female, the names of the Other. In 'Silence: A Fable', the Demon describes the site of terror, in terms which originate in, but significantly differ from, those of Coleridge:

The waters of the river have a saffron and sickly hue; and they flow not onward to the sea, but palpitate for ever and for ever beneath the red eye of the sun with a tumultuous and convulsive motion. For many miles on either side of the river's oozy bed is a pale desert of gigantic water lilies. They sigh one unto the other in that solitude, and stretch towards the heaven their long and ghastly necks, and nod to and fro their everlasting heads. And there is an indistinct murmur which cometh out from among them like the rushing of subterrene water.

Here there is silence, or at best a sound which bears no differentiation. There is also no possibility of escape, because the motion of these waters is in no direction; they are stuck for ever in position no matter how they might heave and boil with frustration.

But, more than that, there are two rivers here: the pinioned river of the surface, the imagined possibility of subterranean 'rushing' below. Poe makes this claim in 'MS. Found in a Bottle': 'I have been all my life a dealer in antiquities, and have imbibed the shadows of fallen columns at Balbec, and Tadmor, and Persepolis, until my very soul has become a ruin.' But this does not help him in the paradox of the two rivers: how can it be that a dual suffering is experienced: that on the one hand there is fear of being becalmed, the fear of motionlessness, while on the other there is the equal terror that, at some other level, everything is passing by, passing away? At neither point, within neither scenario, is there scope for human action; yet it is, I would say, in his descriptions of the static, the ever-repetitive, the inescapable, that Poe comes closest to a realisation of the problem of intensity and narrative.

It is at this peculiar still point, for instance, that the *dénouement* of 'Berenice' begins; it is 'an afternoon in the winter of the year, – one of those unseasonably warm, calm, and misty days which are the nurse of the beautiful Halcyon'. There is something about these surroundings of motionless warmth, the arrested river, which endlessly replays the warmth which preceded exile, and something about the quality of the air in these conditions which renders the memory peculiarly susceptible to an indelible engraving, which is desperately unwanted but which yet cannot be avoided. The same thing happens in 'The Assignation', when the hero gets his first glimpse of the Marchese Aphrodite: 'a snowy-white and gauze-like drapery seemed to be nearly the sole covering to her delicate form; but the mid-summer and midnight air was hot, sullen, and still, and no motion in the statue-like form itself, stirred even the folds of that raiment of very vapor which hung around it as the heavy marble hangs around the Niobe'.

The plot of 'The Assignation' consists of the hero stumbling into knowledge of a relationship between the Marchese and a young man *who remains nameless throughout*. This relationship, although the narrator does not know it, is about to issue in a death-pact, and the narrator is called upon to be an unwitting witness of the suicide of the nameless acquaintance. But the ending is singularly ambiguous, even for Poe: his acquaintance certainly dies, of poison, but not before the narrator himself has drunk of the same wine. I do not mean to suggest that Poe intended this ambiguity; that would be very unlikely. But it still exists, and serves to call into question the relation between these two nameless characters. But, then, the narrator's senses have already been confused by a specific environment, one which mediates in a significant way between the dark heat of 'The Pit and the Pendulum' and the lost and silent warmth of the river:

> Rich draperies in every part of the room trembled to the vibration of low, melancholy music, whose origin was not to be discovered. The senses were oppressed by mingled and conflicting perfumes, reeking up from strange convoluted censers, together with multitudinous flaring and flickering tongues of emerald and violet fire. The rays of the newly risen sun poured in upon the whole, through windows formed each of a single pane of crimson-tinted glass.

Here again is the fear of enclosure, of an environment so total and so undifferentiated that the individual disappears, becomes merely a part of the rich patterns. In this world, breath itself ceases, as it does for the unfortunate M. Valdemar, and as it does again in the quizzical tale called 'Loss of Breath'.

This is written in Poe's lighter mode, and concerns a man who unaccountably ceases to breathe and is therefore consigned to the underworld, although he has no doubts that he is still alive. There he encounters a prodigiously fat man – or rather, the corpse of such a man – and proceeds to meditate upon him:

> He has never ascended the summit of a hill. He has never viewed from any steeple the glories of a metropolis. Heat has been his mortal enemy. In the dog-days his days have been the days of a dog. Therein, he has dreamed of flames and suffocation – of mountains upon mountains – of Pelion upon Ossa. He was short of breath – to say all in a word, he was short of breath.

The story of the 'House of Usher' begins on a 'dull, dark, and soundless day in the autumn of the year, when the clouds hung oppressively low in the heavens'; resolution can come only through the storm and the whirlwind, echoing the other emphasis in Poe on whirlpools, and on the depths they might disclose. Perhaps, after all, what might become apparent at the bottom of the maelstrom, if we can summon our courage, is the way back in: back into the womb, or back into some region where we will be no longer becalmed, stuck in the enclosing heat.

But it would not do, as we see, to attempt too unilateral an interpretation of this configuration of motifs: they are obviously ones which concerned Poe intensely, but the lines of significance are muddled, tied in knots. In 'A Tale of the Ragged Mountains', it is 'upon a dim, warm, misty day, towards the close of November, and during the strange *interregnum* of the seasons which in America is termed the Indian Summer' that Bedloe leaves for his walk in the mountains. In the course of that walk, he finds himself unaccountably transposed into someone else; and on his return from it, he finds it impossible to reinhabit his own body, and dies. The enclosure, the womb, terrify Poe but it is also there that battle has to be engaged, only on that terrain that the struggle for individuation can take place, however prematurely blighted its consequences.

I should like to return to the title of this essay, 'Tales of Dark Heat'. It may indeed seem surprising: for the premature burial theme, for one, is bound up more with images of eternal cold. I hope, however, I have laid out some of the evidence for seeing Poe as preoccupied with a dark heat, the heat of prolonged and pointless tumescence, and at the same time the warmth of an environment which professes simultaneous safety and suffocation, a security unto death. And it was partly because of my interest in this configuration that I chose that title. But this turned out not to be the only reason, although I did not immediately realise the other one.

Bob Dylan's album *Desire* contains only two songs which have sub-titles, and these sub-titles are 'Tales of Old New York' and 'Journey through Dark Heat'. I did not know that I had put these titles together, but clearly I had. And I think there is a further connection: language plays strange tricks with us, as Poe himself would have readily granted, and I believe it is significant that I am trying to describe Poe in terms, precisely, of the 'sub-titles of desire'. In other words, I believe that Poe makes apparent the point that Hegel was the first to underline about the nature of desire, which is that it is endless. There is very little 'desire *for*' in Poe; the movement towards the loved one is invariably blocked, in the

Gothic mode by premature death, in the more comic modes by ridicule or accident. Instead there is the endless circling of desire upon itself, the desire to avoid which must at the same time play constantly with the object of its abhorrence, because to be separated from it would be tantamount to death.

I would suggest, on the basis of this, that reading Poe provides us with a singular experience of ambivalence: birth is feared and needed, the act of naming by which we proceed under the domination of language is longed for yet murderous. This ambivalence is best caught, for me, in the motto which introduces the story 'Ligeia':

And the will therein lieth, which dieth not. Who knoweth the mysteries of the will, with its vigour? For God is but a great will pervading all things by nature of its intentness. Man doth not yield himself to the angels, nor unto death utterly, save only through the weakness of his feeble will.

There are three words which I would call attention to here. First, 'vigour': a significant word, especially when placed alongside the fact that Poe's revenants are for the most part remarkable for their lack of vigour, for the relative failure which attends all these acts of rebirth. The hope is, perhaps, to conjure a new vigour from the depths of abandonment; but this cannot succeed. Second, 'intentness': it is this that I have been trying to get at by talking of Poe's moments of intensity, this longing to bring all the heterogeneous faculties to bear on a single object, lying alongside the concomitant knowledge that, if we bring our faculties to bear in this way, we do not consolidate the image but fracture it, that the body with which we intended to invest the full weight of passion lies, abruptly, in scattered fragments at our feet; or, at the least touch, shows the rot which has in reality been attending it throughout its so-called 'life'. And, third, 'lieth'. I have little doubt that Poe would extrapolate this first sentence into a statement about the strength of the will which lies within all of us if only we can grasp it with intensity and focus ourselves on the evasion of death. But, perhaps, that concept indeed 'lieth' in the other sense, indeed deludes us, figures merely as a permanent evasion of the problems with the will as it actually exists, in all its faultiness and fluctuation. A lie of strength to counteract a lie of weakness: a story woven out of the hopes of survival which turns out to betray the fear of being for ever stuck in an unchanging universe, enclosed in the incomprehensible and misty heat which, in the end, prevents transformation while it encourages us to fill in the gaps with our own imaginary narratives of transcendence.

Notes

1. All quotations from Poe's stories are from *The Complete Works of Edgar Allan Poe*, ed. J. A. Harrison, 17 vols (New York: Thomas Cole, 1902) II–VI. Of the stories discussed here at any length, 'The Cask of Amontillado' can be found in vol. VI, 167–75; 'The System of Dr Tarr and Prof. Fether' in vol. VI, 53–77; 'Berenice' in vol. II, 16–26; 'The Pit and the Pendulum' in vol. V, 67–87; 'The Assignation' in vol. II, 109–24.

2. On puns, see Sigmund Freud, *Jokes and their Relation to the Unconscious* (1905), in *The Standard Edition of the Complete Psychological Works of Sigmund Freud*, ed. J. Strachey, 23 vols (London: Hogarth Press, 1953–73) VIII. See also Freud, *The Psychopathology of Everyday Life* (1901), in *Standard Edition*, VI, 53–105, on 'slips of the tongue'.

3. There is a significant connection here with what happens in Bram Stoker, *Dracula* (1897), and other vampire tales: see David Punter, *The Literature of Terror: A History of Gothic Fictions from 1765 to the Present Day* (London: Longman, 1980) pp. 256–63.

4. See Jacques Lacan, 'The Subversion of the Subject and the Dialectic of Desire in the Freudian Unconscious', in *Ecrits: A Selection*, tr. Alan Sheridan (London: Tavistock, 1977) pp. 292–325.

5. It is also worth here referring to C. G. Jung, *The Psychology of Dementia Praecox* (1907), in *The Collected Works of C. G. Jung*, ed. Herbert Read *et al.*, 20 vols (London: Routledge and Kegan Paul, 1957–79) III, 82–3; and 'The Content of the Psychoses' (1914) in *Collected Works*, III, 163–5.

6. See Lacan, 'The Function and Field of Speech and Language in Psychoanalysis', in *Ecrits*, pp. 30–113.

2
Capitalising on Poe's Detective: the Dollars and Sense of Nineteenth-Century Detective Fiction

CLIVE BLOOM

The classic detective story seems purposely to have been created in order *to avoid* the demands of social realism. In becoming 'simply' escapist literature such detective tales consciously created their own social milieu, half fabulous, half mythical – a milieu so powerful that later generations would comprehend the era in which these tales were written *through* the medium of the tales themselves. In so doing later generations of readers would understand the world of Dupin, Holmes, and so on, to be an actual reflection (a *conscious* mirroring) of social forces at work and at conflict in that period. As such, these tales would have replaced the 'real' world with themselves, interposing themselves within that displacement and creating a new perspective. By interposing between contemporary historical forces and the reader this fiction *denies* its origins and replaces those origins with an enclosed and organised 'world'. This fictional world is a substitute for and not a mirror to social forces, but in its escapist avoidance of historical and social demands detective fiction can clearly be seen to incorporate those very demands it attempts to elide. An escapist and totally fictional landscape denies the 'facts' of its origin.

Strangely, perhaps, that very perspective is a result of the detective tale's being the only fiction that *insists* it is dealing with facts. These facts, however, attested by the many witnesses and clues, and confirmed by both detective and villain, are presented nevertheless as a condition of a 'pure' fiction. Hence everything is at all times *shown* and a theatrical space is opened wherein the effects of a certain *trompe l'oeil* are created. If we turn to Edgar Allan

14

Poe we find the effects of the acrobatic virtuosity of an ourang-outang attested by the extravagant death of two women *displayed* theatrically upon the stage of a locked room and by the auditory account of witnesses from 'the five great divisions of Europe'.[1] Of the ourang-outang Poe says, 'now, how strangely unusual must that voice have really been, about which such testimony as this could have been elicited! – in whose *tones*, even, denizens of the five great divisions of Europe could recognize nothing familiar!' ('The Murders in the Rue Morgue').

Such theatricality is the measure of Poe's social realism too. In 'The Man of the Crowd' Poe gives a long description of a nineteenth-century crowded city. In this description Poe meticulously (and unfavourably) lists the gradations of his society:

At first my observations took an abstract and generalizing turn. I looked at the passengers in masses, and thought of them in their aggregate relations. Soon, however, I descended to details, and regarded with minute interest the innumerable varieties of figure, dress, air, gait, visage, and expression of countenance.

By far the greater number of those who went by had a satisfied business-like demeanor, and seemed to be thinking only of making their way through the press. Their brows were knit, and their eyes rolled quickly; when pushed against by fellow-wayfarers they evinced no symptom of impatience, but adjusted their clothes and hurried on. Others, still a numerous class, were restless in their movements, had flushed faces, and talked and gesticulated to themselves, as if feeling in solitude on account of the very denseness of the company around.... There was nothing very distinctive about these two large classes beyond what I have noted.... They were undoubtedly noblemen, merchants, attorneys, tradesmen, stock-jobbers – the Eupatrids and the common-places of society – men of leisure and men actively engaged in affairs of their own – conducting business upon their own responsibility. They did not greatly excite my attention.

The tribe of clerks was an obvious one; and here I discerned two remarkable divisions. There were the junior clerks of flash houses – young gentlemen with tight coats, bright boots, well-oiled hair, and supercilious lips. Setting aside a certain dapperness of carriage, which may be termed *deskism* for want of a better word, the manner of these persons seemed to me an exact

facsimile of what had been the perfection of *bon ton* about twelve
or eighteen months before. They wore the cast-off graces of the
gentry; – and this, I believe, involves the best definition of the
class.

The division of the upper clerks of staunch firms, or of the
'steady old fellows', it was not possible to mistake. These were
known by their coats and pantaloons of black or brown, made to
sit comfortably, with white cravats and waistcoats, broad solid-
looking shoes, and thick hose or gaiters. – They had all slightly
bald heads, from which the right ears, long used to pen-holding,
had an odd habit of standing off on end. I observed that they
always removed or settled their hats with both hands, and wore
watches.... There were many individuals of dashing appearance, whom I easily understood as belonging to the race of swell
pick-pockets.... I watched these gentry with much inquisitive-
ness.... The gamblers, of whom I descried not a few, were still
more easily recognizable. They wore every variety of dress, from
that of the desperate thimble-rig bully, with velvet waistcoat,
fancy neckerchief, gilt chains, and filagreed buttons.... There
were two other traits, moreover, by which I could always detect
them; a guarded lowness of tone in conversation, and a more
than ordinary extension of the thumb in a direction at right
angles with the fingers.... Descending in the scale of what is
termed gentility, I found darker and deeper themes for speculation.

When Poe's narrator looks at the 'masses' he finds not class but
class as psychology, for 'expressions of countenance' fascinate the
viewer, himself removed, aloof and superior – an adept in
psychological analysis, in the psychology of 'reality'. Nevertheless,
this psychologist, who is himself, ironically, one of the crowd,
guides us through an account rendered *more* acute by its total
disavowal of inner psychological exploration in favour, instead, of
an explanation through an analysis of fashion – that is, an analysis
of appearance. While the delusional state of the narrator advises
the reader's caution (for the narrator is a neurotic with paranoidal
fantasies of 'conspiracy' and fragmentation) in following his
account of the crowd we can say that he is deluded only in as much
as he *totalises* incorrectly – he draws wrong conclusions. His
evidence is, however, *bona fide*.

Thus, the gradations of the crowd present themselves first as spectacle, as *tableaux vivants* and as theatrical pageant. 'All life is here' before the spectator's eyes, and it is for the eyes of the spectator that such a pageant is enacted. In presenting such a slice of contemporary life Poe clearly demonstrates the conservative and reactionary element necessary for detective fiction: everything in its place, everyone in his allotted role. Anything out of that order, *displaced* as it were, will ultimately relate to crime, the social deviancy of crime, and the criminologists who investigate it. (Here we may define deviance as *beyond the limit of the law*. The police only represent the law but criminal and detective are beyond it.)

Poe's realism is, then, counter to the fragmentary and decentred and *disordered* society he actually believed he found himself in. Poe's art is an antidote to contemporary social displacement on a wide scale. His solution is to enumerate the classes through their imitatory functions: a grading on a static–classificatory rather than Darwinian–evolutionary model, dealing not with individuals but with general types regarded as species or grades of humanity (the higher the more developed, the lower the more 'vicious'), with those outcasts the 'Jew Peddler' and the prostitute almost at the bottom, two essential and unmentionable species (of course, it is ironic that at the very end of that list comes the 'old man' and the narrator!). As species, each level is static and functions only to stay in its own position. Each class is 'marked' by its trade and therefore ultimately immobile because always recognisable. Thus, the list resolves itself around the figure of 'the loathsome and utterly lost leper in rags – the wrinkled, bejewelled and paint-begrimed beldame' and social realism resolves itself in pantomime – a pantomime of descending orders of parasites.

I have said that this categorisation is a result of an antidotal procedure on the part of Poe and that the therapeutics of Poe's art are precisely to be found in the unifying and harmonising quality of a genre that leapt upon the scene fully formed in the 1840s. This genre not merely unified within it certain contradictory phases of the period, but also anticipated, through Conan Doyle, a further set of developments dependent upon this first phase. Why then did the detective story form itself quite like this? In what sense is it a product of and an *accurate* reflection of a certain series of moments in the nineteenth century? In what ways does the *art* of the detective story disguise, naturalise and neutralise these contradictions in society so that the contradictions seem no longer to exist and indeed seem *never* to have existed? Let us note before answering these questions that detective fiction answers contradictions by resolution and that in so doing it does not even seem to be addressing a problem about contradictions at all. Here clues are contradictions purposely placed in order to stand for, or obscure, social contradictions. To most readers the detective story is 'pure' escapism designed as a therapeutic avoidance of the problems of everyday existence (the alleged favourite reading of politicians and of readers at bedtime: fiction before the advent of dreams). To whose door do we escape?

It is to that archetypal outsider, the detective, that the representatives of the law have to tramp in order to find their man. And yet, precisely because the detective is an outsider figure, he is more fully integrated into society than those characters who represent society. This is ironic but not unexpected, for in Gogol, Melville, Hawthorne, Conrad and Kafka the outsider is *the* archetypal member of society, represented as the faceless bureaucrat, the businessman, the office clerk, the storekeeper, the representative. Each is singled out because of his very ordinariness. This ordinariness *is* his peculiarity, for each is ultimately a representative of the nineteenth- and early-twentieth-century fear, not of industrialisation, but of bureaucracy: of the 'company man'.

The detective is in this respect no different from each of these characters, in as much as he is ordinary by the very fact of his peculiarity. His 'resolvent' nature makes of him a 'special' everyman figure, and this 'resolvent' ability is emphasised in Poe: 'observing [Dupin] in these moods, I [Poe's narrator] often dwelt meditatively upon the old philosophy of the Bi-Part Soul, and amused myself with the fancy of a double Dupin – the creative and the resolvent' ('The Murders in the Rue Morgue'). Dupin has the resolvent ability of a reader (the detective–reader is an everyman). In this way the detective, like the narrator in 'The Man of the Crowd', is 'invisible' and therefore unacknowledged (the police take the credit publicly) and he becomes a social 'nothing' precisely because he is so needed by society to resolve its various contradictory elements. What then is resolved by the detective, at once outcast, social pariah and yet so needed and so ordinary? Moreover, what is it that makes society suddenly need a 'consulting detective'? (Dupin fulfils this function without explicitly being called one; unlike Holmes, Dupin has *no* social status.)

Let us follow the initial entry of this curious species of investigator into the arena of world literature. Poe's narrator tells us that,

> Residing in Paris during the spring and part of the summer of 18—, I [the narrator] there became acquainted with a Monsieur C. Auguste Dupin. This young gentleman was of an excellent – indeed of an illustrious – family, but, by a variety of untoward events, had been reduced to such poverty that the energy of his character succumbed beneath it, and he ceased to bestir himself in the world, or to care for the retrieval of his fortunes. By courtesy of his creditors, there still remained in his possession a small remnant of his patrimony; and, upon the income arising from this, he managed, by means of a rigorous economy, to procure the necessaries of life, without troubling himself about its superfluities. Books, indeed, were his sole luxuries, and in Paris these are easily obtained.
>
> Our first meeting was at an obscure library in the Rue Montmartre, where the accident of our both being in search of the same very rare and very remarkable volume, brought us into closer communion. We saw each other again and again. I was deeply interested in the little family history which he detailed to me with all that candor which a Frenchman indulges whenever mere self is the theme. I was astonished, too, at the vast extent of his reading; and, above all, I felt my soul enkindled within me by the wild fervor, and the vivid freshness of his imagination. Seeking in Paris the objects I then sought, I felt that the society of such a man would be to me a treasure beyond price.

Here Poe delineates Dupin's character immediately and in total detail. We shall learn little more of his personality in either 'The Purloined Letter' or 'The Mystery of Marie Rogêt'; the classic detective figure is set for good (in this figure is also set his antithesis, the 'gentleman thief').

The only person with the capability and the *leisure* to become this special person is the aristocrat, 'a young gentleman ... of an illustrious family' lent double value by his being (exotically) French (to an American this, in the nineteenth century, is in a sense exoticism) and by his being a 'gentleman', whose very social position at the top of society ensures his powers of mind. Aristocracy, here, means leisure, patience and above all else the power of aloof 'ratiocination'.

Amid the library of his 'grotesque mansion' the aristocrat is both secluded and excluded from the everyday and more mundane social orders represented by 'the Prefect'. Indeed the Prefect, by representing a lost and confused society, suggests by his presence a disdain for a democracy that Poe considered to be the rule of the mob, only capable of functioning under the grip of a repressive, bureaucratic and controlling hand; a hand, moreover, capable only of mechanical adjustment and mechanical manipulation, without the 'finesse' of an aristocratic style capable of detailed and meticulous meditation.

The aristocrat, then, finds no place in a society whose only grasp of order comes via the Prefect and his gendarmes amid the chaos of an urban, metropolitan society (for Poe's orderly gradations represent a society *in chaos*, a society of imitations, fakes, peddlers, prostitutes and villains, some of whom are actually totally 'other', totally animal).

Out of place, and out of time (Dupin may, like Usher, be the last of his line) the aristocracy is the only force capable, by its very exclusion from class division, of uniting (from above) the society that no longer recognises aristocratic status. Such then is Poe's *feudal* attitude: the necessity of a society based upon obligations from the lower ranks to the upper. Like many nineteenth-century thinkers Poe sees the 'genius' as a transcendent, aristocratic, feudal hero. This hero 'secretly' (for he takes no credit) legislates society, adjusts its workings, rectifies its faults, reorganises its syntax. Like Dracula, Dupin performs at night, in secrecy and in darkness.[2] Consequently in 'The Purloined Letter' he tells the Prefect that 'we shall examine [the case] to better purpose in the dark'.

Nineteenth-century ambivalence toward the aristocrat (a man who appears to be without visible means of support, therefore perhaps immoral? Therefore C. Auguste Dupin a singular CAD!) is again reflected in the theology of a certain figure to whom the aristocrat of medieval lore is joined: that is, *the priest*.

Dupin's life is lived in seclusion amid his books like a monk in his *cell* (singularly appropriate in a detective story). We are told that the narrator, in searching for a book of esoteric lore ('a very remarkable volume'), is brought into 'closer communion' with Dupin. Indeed, Dupin is able to 'fathom' the narrator's 'soul'. In 'The Murders in the Rue Morgue' both *'Sacre'* and *'diable'* occur, while in 'The Mystery of Marie Rogêt' the murder takes place on 'the Sabbath'.

Yet this priestlike function goes still further, for Dupin helps out 'G—' the Prefect, an incompetent ruler who goes, just like the owner of the ourang-outang in 'The Murders in the Rue Morgue', to *confess* his incompetence in these matters, matters requiring the therapy of a particularly secular priesthood.

This new secular priesthood that can 'fathom' the souls of other mere mortals is the invention to a great extent of a specific phase of the industrial revolution – it is the coming into being of *the expert*, a man whose technical ability and whose specialised function in the division of labour is to put everything in order through his overview.

Dupin is an expert, a *consultant* whose function is *not* to act but to think. His thoughts move matter and bring matters to a 'head'. The detective is a craftsman and a technician whose ideological function is to *deny* his specialised knowledge in the very act of employing it. This expert is an aristocrat without need of work whose ability in one specific area looks as if it encompasses *all* areas of knowledge. As such the expert denies his role and yet ironically never loses his status. Dupin's 'encyclopaedic' mind, witnessed by his knowledge of everything from rare books to theatricals, associationism and nebular cosmography, assures him of success. In ways that we shall explore later, Dupin is, as an *expert*, indispensable to contemporary society. His skills masquerade as natural rather than learned, for the fictional expert is intuitive and imaginative. He never serves an apprenticeship and as such the expert in detective fiction is the antithesis of the model of the expert in society, having his expertise by right of *nature*, not nurture. Such natural gifts give the expert inordinate power, the power, in fact, to mobilise 'matter' in order to make it *signify*. Dupin is, in this, the greatest of all pre-Holmesian *forensic* experts. Witness his minute, detailed and meticulous consideration of Marie Rogêt's body:

> The corpse, being supposed at the bottom of the river, will there remain until, by some means, its specific gravity again becomes less than that of the bulk of water which it displaces. This effect is brought about by decomposition, or otherwise. The result of decomposition is the generation of gas, distending the cellular tissues and all the cavities, and giving the *puffed* appearance which is so horrible. When this distension has so far progressed that the bulk of the corpse is materially increased without a

corresponding increase of *mass* or weight, its specific gravity becomes less than that of the water displaced, and it forthwith makes its appearance at the surface. But decomposition is modified by innumerable circumstances – is hastened or retarded by innumerable agencies; for example, by the heat or cold of the season, by the mineral impregnation or purity of the water, by its depth or shallowness, by its currency or stagnation, by the temperament of the body, by its infection or freedom from disease before death. Thus it is evident tht we can assign no period, with anything like accuracy, at which the corpse shall rise through decomposition. Under certain conditions this result would be brought about within an hour; under others it might not take place at all. There are chemical infusions by which the animal frame can be preserved *for ever* from corruption; the bichloride of mercury is one. But, apart from decomposition, there may be, and very usually is, a generation of gas within the stomach, from the acetous fermentation of vegetable matter (or within other cavities from other causes), sufficient to induce a distension which will bring the body to the surface. The effect produced by the firing of a cannon is that of simple vibration. This may either loosen the corpse from the soft mud or ooze in which it is embedded, thus permitting it to rise when other agencies have already prepared it for so doing: or it may overcome the tenacity of some putrescent portions of the cellular tissues, allowing the cavities to distend under the influence of the gas.

Here, even the terrain of the female body is made available, at least in thought, to the voyeurism of an expert of death. As an aristocrat of the industrial age, the expert joins the priest in plying a *craft*, in being part of a *select* band (here, only of one). Forensic science is a (re)creative science – an art.

Where the aristocrat and priest meet in the expert there we find the artist: that late-Romantic artist whose temperament, already, exemplified so graphically in Roderick Usher, feeds upon the esoteric, the *outré* and the grotesque. Asked to help reorder society, the detective as artist turns further *in upon himself* and is doubly and stubbornly solipsistic, preferring to rely on the observation of the workings of his own mind: art as psychology (hence Freud?). Thrown upon the observation of his own ego the detective exults in his freedom. Thus Dupin 'the creative' uses the 'whole air of intuition' to solve a crime. But Dupin cares little for the crime *per se*, only for the crime *as that which engages his attention* (throws it in upon itself). The crime is external stimulus to thinking for its own sake, hence 'as the strong man exults in his physical ability, ... so glories the analyst in that moral activity which *disentangles*. He derives pleasure from even the most trivial occupations bringing his talents into play.' The detective's motto is *l'art pour l'art*, but he achieves this in a pure form unlike an actual artist (say Mallarmé), for he *creates nothing*, meditates upon meditation itself and *refuses to need a subject* except as initial stimulus. The detective-*qua*-artist discourses to exercise *pure style*; he operates his craft. To him life is analysis and analysis is a *game*. Moreover life becomes a game of chess or draughts or whist (as in 'The Murders in the Rue Morgue') played for its own sake and for the sake of its psychology and for the sake of a kind of wit. At that moment the legislators of society unable to enforce the law call upon the detective as an 'unacknowledged legislator of the world'.

Yet, and ironically, the Poe-esque detective deals only in death (for he *never meets* a villain in the reader's presence and hence he takes on the villain's creative role too). From death he creates, manipulating cold 'matter' with vibrant mind, becoming both artist and scientist and scientist as artistic genius. Science is *imaginative play*. By analysing the detective becomes a reader of 'hieroglyphics' and yet remains an artist. *Syncretism* becomes his watchword while robbing him of his artistic function, for at the moment of resolution the artist only proves his superiority in semiotics. Art then becomes a form of reading (Dupin 'lives' in *libraries*) and perhaps the clue to artistic 'impotence' in the nineteenth century. Moreover, this impotence becomes pathological as the artistic genius, the artist in search of the 'ideal', comes nearest (as he approaches the 'ideal') to suffering from a 'diseased intelligence' like a 'madman'. Here medicine takes over, robbing the artist of his function, specialising the 'case' of the artist just as the artist attains his ultimate goal, *truth* to his artistic calling. For detection, like priesthood, like art, is a *calling*.

Aristocrat, priest, artist, madman – each needed by society but excluded from it – describe a set of limits and boundaries. To these we must add the last and most important 'aristocrat' in the nineteenth century, belonging as he does to Carlyle's 'aristocracy of moneybags', for now the detective reconciles each previous figure with the *supreme artist of money: the entrepreneurial capitalist*.

Using his capital (his *head*), the detective is dedicated to moving matter by thought. In so doing he is presented with the facts from which in his considerations he forms a coherent hypothesis, from which in turn he makes a 'mental' *leap*. By this leap the detective reveals himself the *arch-speculator* who speculates merely for its own sake. An artist in matters of money, the detective nevertheless begins penniless (an aristocrat) but is brought huge *sums to invest* by the representatives of society (the Prefect). Thus the 'reward' for capturing the murderers of Marie Rogêt soars daily.

It is Dupin's good fortune to know when to intervene and when to arrange a special reward of unnamed vastness with the police chief. Dupin, who works for money (American slang for *du pain* is, of course 'bread' or money), represents a paradox as he works just for the 'love' of it and is obsessed with speculation for its own sake and hence abstracted from money. Indeed Dupin absents himself from the cash nexus even as he becomes its slave.

At once freed from his 'creditors' and exercising a 'rigorous economy' in order *not* to have to recover his family fortune, Dupin always works only for money. Consequently he becomes a form of capital (a *capital* fellow) by associating with the narrator, who talks of 'feeling that the society of such a man would be to [him] a treasure beyond price'. The capitalist names his price as he is excused from any price ('beyond price'). Thus, here the speculator becomes the very symbol of wealth that accumulates as if by magic, on its own and for its own sake. Yet in accumulating it helps pay off the speculator's creditors Le Bon ('Rue Morgue') and the 'Minister D—' ('The Purloined Letter'). Old debts are thus laid to rest, as if they are simply revenge ('The Purloined Letter'), a revenge indeed in which, by invoking the story of Atreus and Thyestes, the Minister becomes a cannibal – the ultimate *consumer*. Moreover, does not Dupin in such a tale finally 'cook' the books so that the Minister buys back his own bond (blackmail is represented by the letter, sign of the 'bond' – the Minister and Dupin may also be 'brothers') at a final and increased rate of interest?

The detective story unites various essential and yet excluded elements of society: the speculator becomes an aristocrat the more he is an expert technician and an artist.

Notes

1. All quotations from Poe are from *The Complete Works of Edgar Allan Poe*, ed. J. A. Harrison, 17 vols (New York: Thomas Cole, 1902) II–VI.

2. Does the appearance of the 'Count' mark the apotheosis of the bourgeois fear of a rampant, leisured class of 'blood-suckers' indifferent to the *moral* necessities of *work*, sexually indiscriminate, bisexual (that is 'debauched') and 'unkillable' (at least a 'fringe' problem: a limit to bourgeois society); killable only by middle-class morality (the 'sign' of the cross), which makes itself quite certain by pinning down its victim with a stake?

3
Figuring out the Signalman: Dickens and the Ghost Story

GARY DAY

The nineteenth century was an age of transition. The old ideas of man, nature and society, although increasingly questioned, had not yet given way to a new intellectual order. As a result 'the normal state of the Victorian mind was one of indecision or suspended judgement'.[1] This uncertainty was not endorsed by the major novels of the period, but it did find expression in what has been called the 'literature of the fantastic'.[2] According to Todorov, the chief characteristic of such writing was that it established, in both the protagonist and the reader, hesitation over whether events in the story had a natural or a supernatural explanation. In this, it corresponded to exactly the kind of doubt that beset the Victorians: namely, whether they should interpret their world from a spiritual or a secular point of view.

One immediate problem with this account is that it doesn't explain why the fantastic, which was so clearly suited to the temperament of the age, should nevertheless be so peripheral to it. Realism, with its emphasis on order, coherence and limitation, was the dominant literary mode, while the fantastic, which was a negation of all these things, existed on the margin. Perhaps it would be more correct to say that, although the Victorians were troubled with uncertainty, they preferred to repress their doubts and cling instead to the view that ultimate truths did exist and that it would be only a matter of time before reason discovered them. The indecision of the age, in other words, was exactly what it tried to repress, and this may explain why fantastic literature was not part of mainstream nineteenth-century writing.

But what precisely is fantastic literature? Todorov's claim that it establishes hesitation, that it suspends or defers meaning, is not sufficient to distinguish it from other forms of writing. Indeed, if Derrida is to be believed, all writing defers meaning to the extent that every signified can also be a signifier, and thus potentially there is no end to the movement of signification. In fact, the harder one tries to define fantasy the more elusive it becomes. Manlove's claim that it should contain 'a substantial and irreducible element of the supernatural'[3] has little in common with Todorov's formulation, whilst Prickett's observation that the staples of nineteenth-century fantasy were 'a dream like atmosphere and a monster'[4] immediately disqualifies such a story as Dickens's 'The signalman' as a fantastic text even though it may be defined as one on Manlove's terms. It is also one in the sense that it generates hesitation, in the Todorovian sense, while at the same time it conforms to Landlow's model of the ghost story, which should reveal 'terrors within a realistically conceived world [where] the narrator is a sceptical person'.[5]

From this it would seem that stories which are classed as fantasy appear to exceed the definition of fantasy; thus it might be more appropriate to talk of fantastic texts rather than of fantasy in general. The difficulty here, however, lies in how a text can be categorised as fantastic without there being some general idea of fantasy which it resembles. The problem may be illustrated by comparing, for example, Bram Stoker's *Dracula* and H. G. Wells's *The Invisible Man* – two stories that are quite different and yet are both classed as fantasy.[6] Of course, there are different types of fantasy, but the question is what these types have in common that make them part of fantastic literature rather than part of realistic literature. To put it another way, how is it that the term fantasy can be divided against itself while at the same time retaining its essential identity? How can it be split into parts and yet remain whole? What this means in effect is that a fantastic story is already fantastic before it can be shown to be fantastic. Kafka's story 'Metamorphosis' is somehow instantly recognisable as fantasy even before it is shown to be such.

The idea of fantasy is pervasive and eludes individual attempts to define it. Like a ghost it is at once there and not there. It is not a positive term, in the sense that it has a definite meaning; rather it seems to function as a space from which various definitions arise. It is a kind of absence which enables individual fantasies to be somehow present. It is not the ghost or vampire *per se* which makes a story fantastic, but the absence, or nothingness, from which they emerge. Their apparent unreality is a reflection of that void; a void which never appears as itself because of the innumerable definitions which seem to give it substance. To say that a text is fantastic and then demonstrate how it is fantastic is a redundant gesture. The reasons do not prove anything, for that the text is fantastic is something that is already known. A story has to be fantastic before it can be discussed as fantastic, and, without anything to demonstrate, the reasons themselves become fantasies, fantasies of demonstration where there is nothing to demonstrate.

Accordingly, the following discussion of 'The Signalman' is not intended to prove that it is a fantastic text; instead the aim is simply to look at it as a text and see how it works as a text.

The story is quite straightforward and concerns a signalman who is visited by a strange figure which always appears before an accident on the line. The signalman describes this uncanny situation to a somewhat sceptical narrator who interprets it first as a delusion and secondly as a coincidence. But the narrator becomes even less sure about what to believe when the signalman is killed, and so he leaves the reader to decide the meaning of what he has seen and heard. Thus the reader's sense of the unexplained mystery may have more to do with the violation of the convention of omniscience than it has to do with 'The Signalman' as a ghost story *per se*. Is it the sequence of events or the narrator's withdrawal which makes 'The Signalman' an eerie tale?[7] Whatever it is, the fact that the reader is offered a choice makes 'The Signalman' an apparently good illustration of Todorov's theory, for he or she hesitates, like the narrator, over the interpretation of the strange events. Do they make more sense from a supernatural or a scientific point of view?

This hesitation is part of a general tension in the story between that which is 'exact' and that which is 'vague'. The exactness lies in the realistic, detailed setting of the tale, and 'exact' itself is used as a term of praise by the narrator. The vagueness, on the other hand, stems from mysterious feelings and a sense that 'something [is] wrong'. It belongs more to the self than to the world. Indeed, it might be argued that 'exact' refers to the 'world' while 'vague' refers to the 'self'.

It is clear that the narrator, from the picture he gives of the signalman's environment, concentrates on the physical objects which he likes to see arranged in an orderly manner and his description of the signalman's box, where everything is in its proper place, has a singularly approving air. The same note is struck when he writes that the signalman, in 'the discharge of his duties ... [was] remarkably exact and vigilant'. However, there is something of a tautology here in that the signalman's duties consist of 'exactness and watchfulness'; they alone 'were what was required of him'. Thus the signalman performs his duty by performing his duty, he is exact by being exact, and this repetition, instead of emphasising the point, merely makes it redundant. A surfeit is created which cannot be accommodated within the tight narrative structure. There are two ways of accounting for this. First, it is not surprising that a part of the story should be tautological when the same is true of the whole, for 'The signalman' is a twice-told tale; the story that is told to the narrator is the same one as he in his turn tells to his readers.[8] Secondly, the description of the signalman's duties might double as a description of the narrator's task, for his entire stance is that of the exact and watchful observer who merely reports what he sees without commenting on it. The point to note, however, is that the tautological description of the signalman's duties blurs rather than clarifies. As such it alerts the reader to the possibility that something which is 'exact' is not necessarily something which is sharp or clear. The narrator may value 'exactness', but the way the word is used in the story seems to undermine its normal meaning and renders it incapable of signifying.

There is also something odd about the narrator's descriptions, for although they are 'exact' it is hard to believe that they are true. At the beginning of the story, for example, the narrator is on top of a deep trench looking down at the signalman, whose 'figure was foreshortened and shadowed', and, although he is no little distance away and has to shade his eyes against 'an angry sunset', he still manages to notice the signalman's manner and his 'flag ... furled round its short pole'. While the details may be 'realistic', the conditions in which they are perceived are not, and this discrepancy immediately casts doubt on the narrator's 'credibility' for the rest of the story. If he is unsure about the signalman, the reader is equally unsure of him. The narrator doubts the signalman even though the latter tells his story in a calm and logical manner, whereas the reader, on the other hand, doubts the narrator *precisely because* his story *is* told in a calm and logical manner. The characteristics of truth have been used to create an illusion – namely, the narrator's discourse – which then tries to determine whether an illusion lies at the heart of the signalman's story. Here again it is possible to see a doubling or a mirroring process. The narrator's discourse, in producing an illusion, strengthens the illusion which the signalman has seen, and suggests that there is only illusion. The main narrative repeats or reproduces the illusion upon which it is commenting and thus creates a surfeit of illusion which breaks down the distinction between appearance and reality on which it depends.

Because 'exactness' either produces an illusion or fails to signify, it becomes opposite to itself as well as to the idea of 'vagueness' against which it is explicitly contrasted. In addition to belonging to the subjective realm, 'vague' also occurs where there is a problem of interpretation, indicated by such phrases as 'as if' and 'as though'. However, since 'exact' has lost its usual sense, the question arises of whether or not the same can be said of 'vague'. It might be argued, for example, that the vague subjective feelings experienced by the narrator gain in intensity and are a better guide to the nature of events than are his attempts to give a rational description of them. His 'sense' that something is wrong is 'irresistible', whereas his interpretations lack conviction and are easily overthrown. In this respect 'vague' suggests certainty. But it is also true that that which is vague fails to 'signify': things only 'seem' or are 'as if'; they are never definite or revealed in their full identity. This aspect of 'vague' links it with the way 'exact' comes to be its own opposite. Thus the two words 'exact' and 'vague' blend into one another even though the text explicitly contrasts them.

The collapse of this difference has two consequences. First, Todorov's criterion of hesitation is no longer applicable to 'The Signalman', and, secondly, without difference there is no meaning. This is particularly important, for the question which haunts the text is, what is the meaning of the signalman's experience? The answer is that there is no meaning, because the text has, by the way it works, collapsed the differences on which meaning depends. Thus, not only is there no meaning, but there is no *possibility* of meaning. The text assumes that there is a meaning, but the way it works shows that there is not. The story is divided against itself but shows no awareness of the split. The apparition does not mean anything; rather, meaning is the apparition.

'Exact' and 'vague' are two words that seem to be both opposite to themselves and to signify more than their usual sense; another is 'figure'. The narrator sees the 'figure' of the signalman and the signalman runs towards the ghostly 'figure ... just outside the blackness of the tunnel'. 'Figure' is thus both person and spectre. In so far as the signalman only ever sees the figure and does not converse with it, it is also related to language. For, as the narrator tells us, the signalman 'had taught himself a language ... *by sight*' (emphasis added). Another meaning of 'figure' has to do with calculation. The signalman 'had also worked at fractions and decimals ... but was a poor hand at figures'. This sense of 'figure' is bound up with calculation, working out a definite answer to a definite problem, and it is significant that the narrator should use the word 'calculation' in the context of interpreting the signalman's experience: 'men of common sense did not allow much for coincidences in making the ordinary calculations of life'. 'Calculation', and by implication 'figure', are thus associated with explanation.

It is clear from this that 'figure' embraces practically every aspect of the story. It is character, spectre, language and explanation. Distinctions, such as those between appearance and reality are abolished; 'figure' is the source of everything and everything is 'figure', without 'figure' actually being anything itself. What it means depends on the context in which it appears, but that individual meaning is always shot through with other meanings; 'meaning' is suspended between contexts. The dominance of 'figure' shows that in trying to explain it the story is also trying to account for itself. 'What does the spectre mean?' the signalman asks. The narrator suggests that it is either an illusion or a coincidence. But an illusion and a coincidence are also figures; explanation is of the same order as that which it tries to explain. Thus any attempt to understand the figure only reproduces it, because of the figurative nature of all understanding. 'The Signalman', in trying to account for the mysterious apparition, spectre or figure merely underlies its ubiquity. Instead of showing that the figure is a freakish, isolated occurrence, the story shows that it is pervasive and general: it proves that the ghost exists for it is itself the ghost.

When the narrator says that the figure is an illusion he is right, but not in the way he thinks. He imagines that if something is an illusion then it does not exist, but the point about 'figure' is that it exists only through illusion. The different meanings of 'figure' in the story mean that it is never fully present in any one of them;

thus in any given context it is always there and not there like an illusion. 'Spectre' means spectre but it also means character, language and calculation, in virtue of the fact that the figure is used to describe them all. Illusion is not therefore an explanation of 'figure', it *is* figure. The same is true of coincidence. It too is not an explanation of 'figure'; it is figure in the sense that other words in the story, with their different meanings, coincide in the word 'figure'. It is their meeting place, their point of convergence.

Besides the question 'What does the spectre mean?' there is the further, implied question which might be phrased, 'Where do the words come from?' The signalman asks the narrator whether the words he used to call him were 'conveyed to [him] in any supernatural way'. Similarly, the narrator notes with a start that the words which the driver used to warn the signalman – 'For God's sake clear the way' – were 'also the words which I myself . . . had attached, and that only in my own mind, to the gesticulations he [the signalman] had imitated'. Like 'figure', the same words are repeated in different contexts. This alters their meaning and prompts the question of their origin. Given the uncanny repetitions and the circumstances in which they are uttered, it is clear that the source of words is not the self. They seem to arise independently of either the narrator or the signalman and to convey more then either intends. The narrator suggests that the repetition of his words is a coincidence, while the signalman believes their source is a supernatural one. The supernatural, however, is the apparition which, by virtue of its being a figure, is linked to language. Thus the answer to the question 'Where do the words come from?' is that they come from language.

This kind of tautology has already been encountered. Here, it suggests that characters are alienated from language yet at the same time determined by it. They are alienated from it in the sense that language appears as something other, a ghostly apparition which escapes definition, and they are determined by it in the sense that they are caught up in a pattern of signification which neither initiated. this has consequences for the idea of story with its assumption of a teller and a tale. The teller is usually in control of his tale, unfolding and elaborating it in order to capture an audience, but here the narrator seems powerless. The spectre speaks through him in the very first words he utters: 'Halloa! Below there!' The narrator thus becomes a mouthpiece for the mysterious apparition, or the figure of language. And, when he says that the repetition of words is a coincidence, this does not mean that coincidence is an alternative source to the supernatural for words. On the contrary, the supernatural, the figure of language, coincides with the narrator to produce the words. The supernatural and coincidence are one and the same thing, for 'figure' is that in which everything coincides. What the figure is, however, is another matter. All that can be said is that like 'fantasy' it is an empty term which somehow enables signification to take place. In this it seems to resemble Derrida's notion of difference, which 'is the production ... of intervals without which the "full" terms could not signify'.[9]

Figure is also bound up with impulse. Both have a powerful effect in the story and neither can be named or identified except as being part of each other. The signalman's occupation is the result of his having given in to youthful impulses: 'He had been ... a student of natural philosophy ... but had run wild ... gone down, and never risen again.' The signalman's descent is physical as well as social, for he hardly ever gets above 'these lower shadows'. In this way physical space is used to indicate social position. The two seem interchangeable and, like other elements of the story, obey the principle of undifferentiation.

The signalman's descent also implies a rejection of reason, for he preferred to 'run wild' rather than pursue his studies as 'a student of natural philosophy'. This youthful indulgence anticipates his later opposition to the rational explanation of his experience by the narrator. By twice overthrowing reason, the signalman establishes impulse as a dominant force, and its irrational character links it with the apparition, which defies all reasonable attempts to explain it. However, since the signalman originally gave in to his impulses, and since impulse and apparition seem to be identified with one another, then it might be argued that the signalman is responsible not only for his social position but also, at least in part, for the apparition itself. It is significant, for example, that the signalman alone is haunted by the spectre, for this suggests that it may be nothing more than a repressed part of himself, returning in an alienated form. And what is this repressed part but reason itself? The spectre on the line, in other words, may not be that which defies rationality, but may *be* rationality revealed, paradoxically, as unknowable.

If the signalman is a product of his impulses, then so too is the narrator – despite his pose as a detached observer. Throughout the story he experiences involuntary sensations which gradually get stronger until he is no longer able to resist them. The sound of the train coming through the tunnel anticipates this, for it is 'an oncoming rush . . . [that] had force to draw me down'. At first the narrator manages to resist 'the slow touch of a frozen finger tracing out my spine', but after that he shows signs of weakening, for he can only do his 'best' against a disagreeable shudder, while later he loses control by 'involuntarily' pushing back his chair, until finally he is 'unable to overcome [his] feelings'. And just as the signal-man's impulses draw him down, so too, it might be argued, do the narrator's. For example, he can give no real reason why he descends the 'rough, zig-zag . . . path' down to the signalman, nor is it ever clear why he should have wanted to talk to the signalman in the first place, especially when he is 'not happy in opening any conversation'. All that is known about the narrator is that he has been 'shut up within narrow limits all his life', which suggests that his new-found freedom is the result of impulse, the sudden breaking of a lifetime's habit.

If the narrator's descent to the signalman indicates, because of its connection with impulse and descent elsewhere in the text, an abandonment of reason, then the gradual rise of his feelings to a point where they become irresistible has to be seen as a justification after the fact. That is to say, his descent *already* implies the triumph of impulse, so any account of how he *later* comes to lose control of his feelings is 'false' in so far as it doesn't acknowledge that that control was never there to be lost. Its very absence is what 'causes' the story, in that it 'causes' the narrator to descend to the signalman. The narrator's attempt to explain the dominance of feeling when feeling is already dominant is rather like the critic's attempt to pin down the notion of fantasy, for that too is already there and it is precisely that ever-present quality which eludes explanation and indeed silently inhabits it. Finally, by charting the gradual growth of impulse until it is a dominant force, the narrator paradoxically imposes a kind of order on it by showing that it follows a logical development. The loss of control thus comes to be a rational development, just as the apparition itself revealed its rationality when considered as the signalman's repressed reason.

Because figure in the form of spectre is indissolubly bound up with impulse – and by extension the unconscious – it might be claimed that it is a signifier of unconscious desire. However, this does not rest easy with the idea that both figure and impulse are inherently, if paradoxically, rational and therefore conscious. The critic's choice between the two interpretations highlights the problem of interpretation in the story. The fact is that choice is an 'illusion'; there is nothing to choose between figure and impulse as either conscious or unconscious because they are both *simultaneously*. Reason is 'unconscious' because it is hidden in the form of the apparition, while impulse is 'conscious' because it is the most dominant and visible force in the story. The narrator's mistake, like the critic's, is to assume that the apparition is either one thing or the other, when, like everything else in the text, it is both.

The double character of everything in the story implies that no one thing has a single identity. The signalman, however, wants to impress upon the narrator that he is 'nothing but what' the latter finds him. He endeavours to be this by telling the narrator his life story. It seems, however, that the signalman is unsure of his past, for he could 'scarcely believe' that he had once been a student. This doubt concerning his past is mirrored in the narrator's own uncertainty. For example, he refers to those 'long and lonely hours of which *I* seemed to make so much', as if he is not sure whether he made so much of them or not. From this it appears that there is doubt not merely whether ghosts exist but even whether the self exists.

The signalman's uncertainty about his own past not only undermines his claim to be nothing but what he appears to be, but also gives him something in common with the narrator. Something else they have in common is their uncertainty about how to act. The signalman knows that the appearance of the spectre means that there 'is danger overhanging somewhere on the line', but he also knows that no one will believe him if he tells them. 'What can I do?' he asks despairingly. The narrator also wants to know how to act after having heard the signalman's story: 'How ought I to act, having become the recipient of this disclosure?' Both situations involve an organised sense of important responsibility. The signalman's torment is that he knows there will be an accident but there is nothing he can do about it, while the narrator, though distressed because he is doubtful whether the signalman can be trusted to carry out his duties properly, is 'unable to overcome a feeling that there would be something treacherous in my communicating what he had told me to his superiors in the company'.

The condition of feeling responsible or guilty for a state of affairs without *actually* being responsible for it is a common one in Dickens's work and it stems from his experience at Warren's blacking factory. It is clear from his writing on this subject that Dickens saw himself as a victim, a gifted and sensitive child abandoned by his parents. However, he also refers to himself as a 'small Cain',[10] as if he were to some extent responsible for the position in which he found himself. It is this contradiction which seems to reappear in 'The Signalman', giving it an autobiographical slant. The signalman's life story strengthens this aspect of the tale because it recalls, in inverted form, Dickens's own career. Instead of rising in the world, the signalman falls, but the opposite is true of Dickens, who fell then rose.[11] Moreover, the *way* the signalman tells his story recalls the manner in which Dickens writes about his experiences at Warren's. Just as the signalman can scarcely believe his own past, so Dickens is amazed by his. 'It is wonderful to me', he writes, 'that . . . no-one had compassion . . . on me.'[12] The reality of his experience is further undermined by his not knowing how long he was at Warren's. 'I have no idea how long it lasted', he says.[13]

Dickens wrote about his time at Warren's in his *Fragment of Autobiography*, which did not appear until after his death with the publication of Forster's biography. It is significant that it is described as a 'fragment', because Dickens found the task of autobiography impossible. He found it easier to tell his own story by telling stories about other people, namely his characters. Dickens's dilemma was that his experience at Warren's drove him to write yet kept him silent on that very subject when it was that he most needed to write about. This contradiction resulted in a failure to realise himself in writing as a direct entity. He is both there and not there in his characters, who signal his presence without ever revealing it, as does the signalman. Apart from his life story and incredulous attitude to his past, the signalman is also like Dickens in being haunted: he is haunted by the spectre as Dickens is haunted by his own shadow in his work. Moreover, the apparition is part of the signalman to the extent that it is associated with his repression of reason, and it also refers to him with its final warning. It is the latter which baffles the signalman and prompts the question, 'What does the spectre mean?' It means himself, but this is not something he is able to recognise. Neither, strangely, is Dickens able to recognise his own self in the 'mirror' of his work. His characters may have names which sound like his own and they may endure situations similar to the one he endured, but there is no sense of recognition that it is himself he is writing about.

This inability to recognise the self implies that it is split. Certainly this is the case in the *Fragment of Autobiography*, where Dickens is both criminal and victim, and is unable to come to terms with the former or reconcile it with the latter. It is also split in his fiction where different characters represent different parts of his personality.[14] The signalman, too, is divided and cannot see that the apparition is in fact himself. These self-divisions, together with the doubt surrounding the self's past, reduce the self so that it is neither wholly present nor wholly absent, like the apparition.

The split self generates the quest for meaning which would cease if the various parts of the self were brought into harmony with one another. However, as meaning is articulated upon the dualism of either/or, it can only perpetuate the very split it is trying to heal. It might be argued that not only 'The Signalman' but all Dickens's work overcomes this problem through repetition. That is to say, if the self cannot be made whole because meaning demands it be either one thing or the other, then repetition at least gives the fragmented self some kind of continuity, if not unity. However, there is more than a suggestion that the division of the self is 'deliberately' maintained. Perhaps Dickens 'refused' to continue the *Fragment of Autobiography* in case it revealed something about himself which he did not wish to know, something to do with his being a 'small Cain'. The idea of refusing to see is present in 'The Signalman' in the 'as though's and 'seem's which characterise the narrator's prose and have the effect of making the physical world less substantial than a first reading might suggest, and in the recurrent image of figures who cover their eyes. If the physical world, as well as the self, is less substantial, then the apparition is no longer an oddity in it but typical of it. It is this which the figures who cover their eyes cannot or rather refuse to see, and this refusal undermines the implicit claim of the story that there are things which cannot be explained. Of course nothing can be understood if it isn't first examined.

Only one character does not cover his eyes and that is the signalman himself. Furthermore, his words, in contrast to the narrator's, are 'well chosen',[15] and these two features indicate that he is the seeing, articulate centre of the text. This means not that he sees and understands the apparition, but that he is the 'clue' to unravelling the narrator's interpretative problem. The narrator, in other words, should learn from the signalman's experience. The signalman fails to recognise that what the apparition signifies is himself. After his death, the narrator relates the story and in so doing alters the position of the various characters. Where before the apparition was a strange mystery for the signalman, the signalman has now become a strange mystery for the narrator. However, this shift in position has created the possibility of knowledge, for the narrator ought to realise that, if the spectre pointed towards the signalman, then the signalman must point towards him. Repetition of the tale thus threatens to lay it bare and this may explain why the many repetitions in the story are so disturbing. 'The Signalman' may claim that there are things which cannot be known, but its structure shows that the opposite is true. This suggests that knowledge is repressed which echoes somewhat the signalman's abandonment of his studies.

The movement towards and away from knowledge in the story is inscribed in the dialectic between those who see and those who don't. The signalman 'sees' but doesn't realise what he sees – that can only be articulated by repeating his story – while the narrator and the spectre are both shown with their hands covering their eyes. What the narrator doesn't see is the spectre – a figure with whom he has much in common. To begin with he uses the very words that the signalman used: 'Halloa! Below there!' Further, when the signalman is telling the narrator about his experience, the latter twice interrupts him as the ghostly vibration of the bell had twice interrupted him the previous evening.

There also appears to be a resemblance between the spectre and the narrator, for the signalman very nearly mistakes the latter for the former when he says 'I was doubtful ... whether I had seen you before.' The narrator also returns three times to the signalman's box, which is the same number of times the apparition appears at the mouth of the tunnel, and, finally, with the narrator as observer, there may be a play of 'spectre' and 'spectator'. In trying to argue away the apparition, therefore, the narrator is actually concealing himself. He refuses to 'see', in the sense of recognise, his reflection in the spectre.

Moreover, in so far as the apparition is also a figure, the narrator is unable to acknowledge that he too is figuratively constituted, but that is exactly what he is. The word 'figure' in the story embraces the apparition, the signalman, the narrator, explanation, seeing and language, and thus forms a battleground of conflicting meanings – as indeed does the narrator, who is part of the very thing whose existence he questions. It is possible to argue that the narrator's position *vis à vis* the spectre is not dissimilar to Dickens's *vis à vis* his characters, for he too is figuratively constituted by that which he does not recognise as himself. Perhaps this failure to recognise the self stems from the *Fragment of Autobiography*, where the self is split, unseeing and unseen. It exists in a fragmented state through out Dickens's work. This suggests that the flawed autobiography is, in a sense, more 'true' than a complete one: that is to say, the *Fragment* is not a failed autobiography but a successful one, precisely because it is a fragment; and fragmentation, through the medium of his characters, was the only way in which Dickens could satisfy the contradictory need to write his life story without revealing the identity of its hero.

The way in which everything 'means' both more and less than itself in 'The Signalman', the way in which everything coincides or interpenetrates with everything else, may be explained by the character of the *Fragment*. There too everything seems to run into everything else; the young Dickens is both victim and criminal, but there is no sense of any contradiction between the two and the result is the problem that arises also in 'The Signalman': namely, that of feeling responsible for a state of affairs without actually being responsible for them.[16] The convergence of conflicting meanings on one point perhaps signifies a desire for unity.[17] However, this unity is not to be understood as the harmonious organisation of the self; rather it should be seen as the self partaking of every element without those elements ever forming a whole in which the self may see its reflection. Thus in 'The Signalman' the narrator, the signalman and the spectre are all part of one another but none of them 'recognises' himself in the others. Another way of putting this is to say that they all 'play' one another, making it impossible for the reader to decide where the 'real identity' resides, just as the huge cast of Dickens's characters 'play' him and in so doing keep him from view.

The desire for unity is capable of many interpretations. It could, for instance, be seen as the incest fantasy. The trouble is, however, that it could equally be seen as an example of the death wish or the homosexual fantasy, for they are all concerned with the abolition of difference, which is yet another aspect of fantastic literature. However, if 'The Signalman' is concerned with the abolition of difference it is equally true that it maintains difference, and in this respect it undermines, rather than furthers, the notion of fantasy.

With the word 'figure' occupying all the possible positions of signification in the story the reader can find no point of entry into the text. This situation is similar to Dickens's other works, where he endeavours to be both author and reader. As J. Hillis-Miller has noted, Dickens 'wanted to be both actor and spectator, both character and witnessing narrator'.[18] This exclusion of the reader suggests that he or she is some kind of threat. If this is the case, then he or she is rather like the apparition against which the narrator takes a defensive stand. For just as the spectre, by a chain of associations, ultimately points to the narrator, so too the reader has some kind of access to the narrator which must be guarded against. This defensive nature of the text is hard to reconcile with claims that fantasy is the literature of subversion and of the expression of forbidden desires. In the case of 'The Signalman', if forbidden desires are at work in the thrust to unity, the reader is not allowed to see what they mean or from where they come, for this would be to recognise the apparition behind the narrator which refuses to recognise itself. It inhabits a close, rigidly defined world which is not the usual world of fantasy, where boundaries are crossed and limits continually challenged.

The concentration of the different meanings on a single point is one factor of 'The Signalman'; another is repetition. For example, the narrator repeats his request to speak to the signalman – 'I repeated my enquiry' – and the engine driver repeats the words that the narrator had attached to the signalman's gestures: 'For God's sake, clear the way!' The story itself is repeated, for the signalman tells it to the narrator, who then tells it to his readers. Apart from these internal and structural repetitions there is the fact that 'The Signalman', in its paradoxical abolition and retention of difference, and in its eponymous hero's dilemma of feeling responsible without being responsible, repeats the narrative complexities of Dickens's other work.

There seem to be a number of effects of repetition in the story. To begin with, it reinforces the idea of vague but powerful impulses, for as these recur but are unknown, so too repetition recurs without its being known what is being repeated. Repetition may be regarded as the impulse of the story in the sense that it carries it along. However, as everything can be shown to be a repetition of something else, the narrator of the signalman and the signalman of the apparition, it is difficult to find the original thing that is being repeated. It may be, in fact, that nothing is being repeated; there is only the demonic nature of repetition itself, arbitrary and indefinite.

In so far as characters repeat one another's words and gestures, repetition helps to break down the unity of the self. With the self existing in a fragmented state it is unable to recognise those parts of itself that it encounters; hence the signalman is unable to see himself in the apparition. This aspect of repetition serves Dickens's desire to disguise himself in his work.

Another aspect of repetition is that it signifies a failure to progress. The narrator, for example, fails to exploit the possibility of knowledge provided by his repetition of the signalman's tale. Instead of realising that the latter somehow refers to him, he remains as mystified over the signalman as the signalman was over the apparition, which was, in part, his own repressed self. This internal repetititon matches 'The Signalman' as an external repetition of Dickens's other work, and it suggests some unresolved conflict perhaps going even further back than the novelist's time at Warren's.

One of the most important functions of repetition generally is the way it establishes a signifying sequence. Here it appears under the name of 'iterability' and, as Culler notes, something 'can be a signifying sequence only if it is iterable, only if it can be repeated ... in various contexts'.[19] What is repeated, not only in 'The Signalman' but also throughout Dickens's work, is the self as signifier but without a signified. The frantic signalling of Dickens's characters is intended to focus attention on the display, not on what is displayed. Thus the apparition captures the reader's gaze and its extravagant manners force him or her to ask, along with the signalman, 'What does it mean?' This question isolates it from the other figures in the story to whom it is related, and so its 'meaning' is deferred indefinitely. It would be better to ask not what it means, for meaning is illusion, but how it signifies, for that at least draws attention to the way it is bound up with those things from which questions of meaning attempt to separate it. Repetition in this tale does not establish a signifying sequence *per se*, but it does, by placing the signalman in the position of the apparition, establish the irreducible nature of the signifier.

How, therefore, does 'The Signalman' fit in with various notions of fantasy? It would not be hard to show that many elements of the story, such as the uncanny appearance of the spectre, are fantastic, but, as stressed at the beginning, the text is somehow already fantastic before its fantastic characteristics can be listed. Furthermore, it is possible to discover fantastic characteristics in a text which is not fantastic. If fantasy is defined as the indefinite deferral of meaning, then 'The Signalman' is not part of fantastic literature, for there is no meaning for it to defer. Meaning in the story is articulated upon the distinction of either/or, but, as the text collapses this distinction through its play on vagueness and exactness, the very possibility of meaning is removed. Having said this, however, it is also true that knowledge relating to the self is repressed in the image of figures' covering their eyes and in the way the various fragments of the self are somehow kept apart. Once more this puts 'The Signalman' at some distance from fantasy, where the general assumption is that things cannot be known. Here there is a suggestion that things are known and for that very reason they are suppressed. There are even difficulties if it is claimed that 'The Signalman' belongs to fantastic literature because its subject is a mysterious apparition. For, as has been said, the doubt surrounding the spectre extends to the self and to the world the self inhabits, so that the ghost actually becomes the most 'realistic' representation of self and the world instead of being an anomaly. And, if the spectre is suddenly an index of normality, then the narrator himself becomes mysterious because his motives for visiting the signalman are never declared.

If it is impossible to reconcile 'The Signalman' with notions of fantasy it may be because it leans too heavily on Dickens's other works, which, though not part of fantastic literature, nevertheless contain elements of fantasy. The connection with Dickens's other work opens up 'The Signalman' to a possible psychoanalytic reading which would concentrate on how Dickens is disguised and displayed in his work and on the desire for unity. The fragmentation of the self that this implies allows him to deal with an unspecified guilt without recognising it as his own. The problem is, however, that this guilt is perpetuated precisely because it goes unrecognised. Perhaps, then, it might be argued that the perpetuation of guilt amounts to a deferral of the moment when self coincides with self, so that 'The Signalman', in reproducing the pattern of Dickens's other work, is concerned with the suspension of meaning after all. The problem with this is that there is really no self to coincide with other selves, for, as can be seen in 'The Signalman', characters are so like one another that it is impossible to talk of an original self which will unite with its fragmented reflections. There is only the ubiquitous 'figure', which has no meaning itself but is the place where all meanings coincide. It is thus, in itself, an illusion, an empty space on which everything converges. It is also, perhaps, the figure of Dickens, who, like the spectre, is the object of much inquiry. But the figure only enables signification; it is not its goal, which, when reached, anchors it with meaning. It is pure fantasy in the sense that it is not there. Nor, indeed, is Dickens. Yet, like the figure in 'The Signalman', he is everywhere, suspended between presence and absence.

Notes

1. Walter Houghton, *The Victorian Frame of Mind* (New Haven, Conn.: Yale University Press, 1957) p. 20.
2. This seems to be a generally accepted description. See, for example, Rosemary Jackson, *Fantasy: The Literature of Subversion* (London: Methuen, 1981); Tzvetan Todorov, *The Fantastic: A Structural Approach to a Literary Genre* (Ithaca, NY: Cornell University Press, 1975); R. C. Schlobin (ed.), *The Aesthetics of Fantasy Literature and Art* (Notre Dame, Ind.: University of Notre Dame Press, 1982); S. Prickett, *Victorian Fantasy* (Brighton: Harvester Press, 1979); C. N. Manlove, *Modern Fantasy: Five Studies* (Cambridge: Cambridge University Press, 1975).
3. Manlove, *Modern Fantasy*, p. 1. All quotations from 'The Signalman' are from *A Supernatural Omnibus*, ed. Montague Summers (Harmondsworth: Penguin, 1976).
4. Prickett, *Victorian Fantasy*, p. 14.
5. G. P. Landlow, 'And the World Became Strange', in Schlobin, *The Aesthetics of Fantasy Literature*, p. 138. See also David Seed, 'Mystery in Everyday Things: Charles Dickens' "The Signalman" ', in *Criticism*, 23 (Winter 1981) 42–57, which also discusses the story from this point of view.
6. Rosemary Jackson cites both these examples as fantastic texts (*Fantasy*, pp. 22 and 118–22).
7. The convention of the omiscient narrator was at its height during the nineteenth century. The narrator was a sort of father-figure, controlling and guiding his readers and telling them what to think about his characters. The reader was thus dependent on the narrator, so that, when the latter withdrew, the former was bound to be somewhat disoriented. Perhaps it is this loss of a father-figure that jolts the reader of 'The Signalman', so used, as he or she is, to being 'looked after' by nineteenth-century narrators. But, if the father-figure has vanished, he still haunts the text in the form of its

tight construction. The explanation of events may be absent, but their organisation becomes more evident because of it.

8. It might be objected that the death of the signalman makes the narrator's story different from the one he heard from the dead man. However, both stories are still the same to the extent that the original problems of whether the apparition was there and, if it was, what it meant, are still unresolved. It is the story as problem which is retold.

9. Jacques Derrida, *Positions* (Chicago: University of Chicago Press, 1981) pp. 38–9.

10. Quoted in John Forster, *The Life of Charles Dickens* (London: Chapman and Hall, 1874) I, 35.

11. It is a characteristic of Dickens that one of the ways in which he signifies his presence in a work is through a simple reversal. For example if the initials of 'David Copperfield' are reversed, they become C. D., Charles Dickens. He also appears in his novels, at least the early ones, through the names of his characters. 'Pickwick', 'Twist' and 'Nickleby', for instance, are all phonetically similar to Dick-ens. Moreover, it is not just the echo of a name but also that of an 'I' buried in a fictional counterpart.

12. Quoted in Edgar Johnson, *Charles Dickens: His Tragedy and Triumph* (Harmondsworth: Penguin, 1977) p. 33.

13. Quoted in Jack Lindsay, *Charles Dickens: A Biographical and Critical Study* (London: A. Dakers, 1950) p. 60.

14. Oliver, for example, 'represents' Dickens the helpless child in need of care and protection, while the demonic Quilp 'represents' Dickens the man of intense energy and black humour.

15. The narrator cannot remember the words he used when he called down to the signalman ('I cried something to the effect'), nor is he even sure what he spoke to the signalman about ('those long and lonely hours of which I seemed to make so much').

16. The convergence of contradictory things is represented in Dickens's novels chiefly through animism, where animate objects are assimilated to inanimate ones and *vice versa*.

17. The *Fragment of Autobiography* is absolutely crucial to an understanding of Dickens's work. Many of the phrases in it are borrowed straight from his early fiction, so that the distinction between autobiography and fiction is never clear. One thing, however, is certain and that is that both the *Fragment* and the novels, with their crowded claustrophobic atmospheres, are shot through with what may loosely be termed a desire for unity. This might be interpreted as an incestuous desire, and such an interpretation certainly pays dividends when considering the *Fragment*.
    When Dickens refers to himself as a 'small Cain', whom does he imagine he has murdered? To his conscious mind he has murdered no one, but his insistence on innocence itself betrays a sense of guilt, which rather suggests that he felt he had been sent to Warren's as a punishment. But for what? Dickens's close relationship with his mother, attested to particularly by Jack Lindsay, is relevant here. In

other words, Dickens's obscure guilt which befogs his account of Warren's is an Oedipal guilt. But because he either cannot or will not face this guilt, he reproduces, in his mode of narration, the very conditions which brought it about in the first place. That is to say, the 'original' desire for unity which somehow led to his being placed in Warren's reappears in the breakdown of distinctions which characterise his writing about Warren's: for in the breakdown of distinctions meanings collapse and mingle together in one heterogeneous mass. This is also true of the novels and short stories, where animism is one of the many techniques used to undermine distinctions and bring together things which would normally be separated. Thus the 'fiction' replays the *Fragment*, which replays the Oedipus, and this sense of replaying a psychic trauma may account for the vivid immediacy so characteristic not only of Dickens's work but also of the transference relationship.

18. J. Hillis-Miller, 'The Sources of Dickens' Comic Art', *Nineteenth Century Fiction*, 24 (1970) 467–76.

19. J. Culler, *On Deconstruction: Theory and Criticism After Structuralism* (London: Routledge and Kegan Paul, 1982) p. 120.

4

Wilkie Collins in the 1860s: the Sensation Novel and Self-Help

NICK RANCE

Recent manifestations of critical interest in Collins have not tended to impugn his traditional status as a minor novelist, to be mentioned in the same breath as Reade. Feminist criticism has played off a male and reactionary Collins against enlightened female sensation novelists. Elaine Showalter pronounces the novels of Collins in the 1860s to be 'relatively conventional in terms of their social and sexual attitudes'.[1] A misreading is first adduced in evidence. 'The first sentence of *The Woman in White* announced Collins' endorsement of Victorian sex roles: "This is the story of what a Woman's patience can endure, and what a Man's resolution can achieve."'[2] The first sentence, however, is Walter Hartright's as editor of the various narratives, including his own, and announces Hartright's endorsement of Victorian sex roles, but not that of Collins. That Collins was conventional in his sexual attitudes might seem a curious charge to lay against the creator of Marian Halcombe and Lydia Gwilt. Admittedly, the spirited Marian in *The Woman in White* has on her upper lip down which to Hartright is 'almost a moustache' (p. 58). But no less objectionable to Hartright because no less suggestive of an aura of manliness are the qualities revealed in her expression, qualities which Hartright would find admirable in a man. Hartright is incited to assert what has been affronted, his own and the conventional ideal of femininity:

> Her expression – bright, frank and intelligent – appeared, while she was silent, to be altogether wanting in those feminine attractions of gentleness and pliability, without which the beauty of the handsomest woman alive is beauty incomplete.

> (pp. 58–9)[3]

The Italian, Count Fosco, conceives a passion for precisely the attributes which repulse the English drawing-master. Sue Lonoff in her recent book is not intent on exalting female sensation novelists at the expense of Collins, but can still state that 'Collins had no greater ambition than to be a popular novelist – popular in the double sense of selling widely and of appealing to middle-brow, middle-class readers.'[4] The undoubted appeal of the novels to middle-brow, middle-class readers, though not exclusively to such readers, did not stop Collins from being master of a suspense in which what for the reader was suspended was faith in the validity of successive aspects of mid-Victorian orthodoxy. I shall be concerned here not with sexual attitudes in the fiction, which have been the focus of much of the new critical interest in Collins, but rather with the fictional project of undermining the traditional bourgeois ethic of self-help.

Serialised from November 1859 to August 1860 in *All the Year Round*, *The Woman in White* inaugurated a decade of literary sensationalism. In the 1860s, Collins is a historical novelist preoccupied by the very recent past. All four of the novels published in the 1860s, *The Woman in White*, *No Name*, *Armadale* and *The Moonstone*, are set in England in the late 1840s and, except for *No Name*, the early 1850s. At the beginning of his autobiography, *The Life and Adventures of George Augustus Sala* (1895), Sala, who knew Collins from *Household Words* days, wrote of the International Exhibition of 1862 that

> the display presented two conspicuous departures from the lines laid down in 1851. In that year, no modern weapon of war was to be seen in the palace of glass and iron. In 1862 section after section showed cannon, gun, muskets, rifles, pistols, swords, daggers, and other munitions of warfare. The promoters of the First Exhibition had thought, good souls! that the thousand years of war were over, and that the thousand years of peace were to be inaugurated; but they had awakened from that dulcet dream in 1862. Solferino and Magenta had been fought, and the great American Civil War was impending.

Margaret Oliphant, whose essay 'Sensation Novels' appeared in *Blackwood's Magazine* in May 1862, explained the new literary school in terms of the *Zeitgeist*: 'it is natural that art and literature should, in an age which has turned out to be one of events, attempt a kindred depth of effect and shock of incident'. Like Sala, Oliphant was impressed by the contrast between the mood of the 1860s and the optimism of 1851: 'we who once did, and made, and declared ourselves masters of all things, have relapsed into the natural size of humanity before the great events which have given a new character to the age'. Margaret Oliphant was thinking of wars abroad and particularly the American Civil War:

> That distant roar has come to form a thrilling accompaniment to the safe life we lead at home. On the other side of the Atlantic, a race *blasé* and lost in universal *ennui* has bethought itself of the grandest expedient for procuring a new sensation; and albeit we follow at a humble distance, we too begin to feel the need of a supply of new shocks and wonders.

Oliphant may be suspected of being disingenuous in contrasting thrilling America with safe England. The English fascination with events in America was because the war seemed provoked by something more urgent than *ennui*. As did the English monied classes generally, *The Times* supported the South, because it was assumed to be rebelling against democracy. In the 1860s, with the emergence of an organised union movement and vigorous campaigns for reform of the franchise, democracy was a prospect much contemplated in England. The Civil War was a terrible warning which English democrats would do well to heed: it certainly encouraged their opponents to think that the triumph of democracy was not inevitable. Reviewers stressed the contemporaneity of setting of sensation novels as a distinctive feature of the school, and H. L. Mansel, in a marathon review of sensation literature, explained that it was necessary to be near a mine to be blown up by the explosion (*Quarterly Review*, Apr 1963). Unlike most of his emulators, however, whose opening chapters are indeed set three or four years back to allow the plot to culminate in the present, Collins was exploring the prehistory of the mood of crisis in the 1860s. The sensational plots of *The Woman in White* and *Armadale* culminate in what Lydia Gwilt in *Armadale* sacrilegiously refers to as 'the worn-out old year eighteen hundred and fifty one' (p. 496). Like some recent historians of his age, Collins was denying even the briefest period of mid-Victorian 'calm'.

Margaret Oliphant commented in her review on the completeness with which the domestic saga had been superseded in public favour by the sensation novel. She complimented Collins on being the first novelist since Scott to keep readers up all night over a novel:

> Domestic histories, however virtuous and charming, do not often attain the result – nor, indeed, would an occurrence so irregular and destructive of all domestic proprieties be at all a fitting homage to the virtuous chronicles which have lately furnished the larger part of our light literature.

Oliphant not only shared a London house with Dinah Mulock, author of the bestseller *John Halifax, Gentleman*, than which no domestic saga is more virtuous, but also during the vogue for the saga herself produced five domestic novels between 1854 and 1860. *The Athelings* was published in 1857. The heroine, Marian, 'had heard of bad men and women', but nevertheless, 'safe as in a citadel, dwelt in her father's house, untempted, untroubled, in the most complete and thorough security'. Meredith wryly reflected on what constituted the appeal to the public of *The Athelings*. 'The secret is that the novel is addressed to the British Home, and it seems that we may prose everlastingly to the republic of the fireside . . . .' The first domestic saga, Bulwer's *The Caxtons*, was serialised in 1848 and 1849, and the vogue ran through the 1850s. This was also the period of the acme of popularity of Martin Tupper's versified edification. Originally published in 1838, *Proverbial Philosophy* in the tenth edition appeared in 1850, and in the thirty-eighth in 1860. There was no thirty-ninth edition until 1865. According to Gladstone, Tupper was 'slain' by an article in the *National Review* in July 1858, calling him 'a kind of poetical Pecksniff' with the 'motto, "my friends, let us be moral"'. The placidity which Oliphant suggests as characterising domestic sagas would imply them to be the literature of an age of equipoise. Superficial placidity, however, is at odds with the underlying neuroticism of the sagas. E. J. Hobsbawm has remarked how 'the structure of the bourgeois family flatly contradicted that of bourgeois society. Within it freedom, opportunity, the cash nexus and the pursuit of individual profit did not rule.'[5] Domestic moralism has its counterpart in the public sphere in Smilesian moralism, and the virtuous practices inculcated in the home are alleged to be a recipe for social success, but the felt inadequacy of the home as a social model keeps breaking through in the sagas. However idyllic the British Home, to emerge from the portals is dangerous, even if only for children to marry and launch another domestic idyll. The principle is grudgingly conceded in *John Halifax, Gentleman*: 'it was but right that Nature's holy law should be fulfilled – that children, in their turn, should love, and marry, and be happy, like their parents'. But the plots of the domestic sagas show that the concession is indeed grudging. There is a prevalence of marrying cousins and thereby not disrupting the original family circle, of daughters who stay at home and never marry, and of children who escape the horns of the dilemma by dying young, like Muriel in *John Halifax, Gentleman*. Ethel May, in Charlotte Yonge's *The Daisy Chain*, excels in virtue by cheerfully relinquishing a romance with a cousin, Norman May, who has, however, a 'brilliant public career', which is suspect in itself.

The agoraphobia of *John Halifax, Gentleman* is the more extraordinary since Halifax is supposed to be exemplary Smilesian man. Having arrived in Norton Bury a penniless urchin, Halifax is employed in Mr Fletcher's tanner's yard. Eventually, he is refusing nominations as a parliamentary candidate and living in Beechwood Hall, though the moral is obscured by his persistently hinting at his gentle birth. This subverts the propaganda mission of the novel, since it is not clear whether his virtues are those which any working man may emulate or whether they derive from the birth which gives the title 'gentleman', traditional rather than Smilesian connotations. Other working men in the novel are presented as a confused mob. When debating Halifax's status, however – 'No, he be a real gentleman' – 'No, he comed here as poor as us' – the mob is precisely as confused as the novel. Mulock's ideological tangle extends to the Fletchers, Phineas's father anticipated Halifax by arriving in Norton Bury 'without a shilling in his pocket' and rising to become a large employer. Fletcher, however, is invariably conscious that he 'originally came of a good stock': he names his son 'after one of our forefathers, not unknown – Phineas Fletcher, who wrote the "Purple Island"'.

Mulock palpably lacks confidence in the Smilesian ethic which her novel was famous for celebrating. Like nearly all Smiles's encouraging examples in *Self-Help*, *John Halifax, Gentleman* is back-dated to the 'heroic age' of self-help, the late eighteenth and early nineteenth centuries. Rather than being imperialistic, however, on behalf of domestic moralism, the novel is neurotically defensive; desiderata are quietness, passivity and staying at home – even dying at home, which is a permanent staying. Whereas Smiles himself included 'energy' in his list of cardinal virtues, merely to be adult in *John Halifax, Gentleman* is to be in crisis. The devotion between John and his wife proceeds from childhood and remains childlike. Their sons, Edwin and Guy, are less fortunate. They simultaneously fall in love with the governess, who has suppressed her French paternity and more specifically that her father was 'D'Argent the Jacobin – D'Argent the Bonnet Rouge'. The Jacobinical aura of the governess reflects her status as ardent young woman in the house. She is not romantically culpable and respectably marries Edwin. Guy, however, whom she has not encouraged, moves 'away into the wide, dangerous world'.

In 1867, reviewing fiction by the second generation of female sensation novelists, Margaret Oliphant remarked that 'the last wave but one of female novelists was very feminine. Their stories were all family stories, their troubles domestic, their women womanly to the last degree, and their men not much less so. The male characters in Bulwer's domestic sagas, it may be remarked, are no less 'womanish' than those of Mulock or Yonge. Female sensation novelists, Oliphant complained, had so far erred in the other direction as to mould their 'women on the model of men, just as the former school moulded its men on the model of women'. Halifax's youthful yearning for Ursula reduces him to the sick-bed, though his suit is so far from unpromising that Ursula promptly consents to marry the invalid. The highest compliment Phineas can pay to the blind Muriel Halifax, who dies as a child, is that 'she was better than Joy – she was an embodied Peace'. The eulogy continues, 'everywhere and always, Muriel was the same. . . . The soft dark calm in which she lived seemed never broken by the troubles of this our troublous world.' Muriel's death then prompts Halifax's temporary failure to fulfil his early promise: 'all the active energies and noble ambitions which especially belong to the prime of manhood, in him had been, not dead perhaps, but sleeping'. Halifax himself dies at the early age of fifty-four.

As a sensation novelist, Collins was both conscious of and scathing about the preceding fashion in popular fiction. Lydia Gwilt in *Armadale* abuses 'nauseous domestic sentimentalists'. Having engaged to impart her full story to Midwinter before their wedding, she readily invents her 'little domestic romance'. 'There was nothing new in what I told him', she admits in her diary: 'it was the commonplace rubbish of the circulating libraries'. Charlotte Yonge's *The Heir of Redclyffe*, the cult of which in domestic circles was rivalled only by that of *John Halifax, Gentleman*, provoked a virulent though belated review by Collins. 'The characters by whose aid the story is worked out, are simply impossible. They have no types in nature, they never did have types in nature, and they never will have types in nature....' Setting his sensation novels in the period in which the domestic sagas flourished, Collins foregrounds the sense of unease which disrupts the pose of complacency of the sagas. The moral of the sagas generally, as it is pronounced by Pisistratus Caxton to be that of Bulwer's *My Novel*, might be that 'Conduct is Fate'. The sagas are evidently less than confident about this, since they turn away from the world to which domestic morality is supposed to hold the key. There is a telling compliment to the poetical Leonard Fairfield's wife in *My Novel* that, 'if the man's genius made the home a temple, the woman's wisdom gave to the temple the security of a fortress'. At least in so far as 'conduct' has the intended moral connotations, the sensation novels of Collins obdurately dispute the premise that 'Conduct is Fate'.

What one might call with Margaret Oliphant the first 'sensation scene' of *The Woman in White* (Oliphant borrows the term from the contemporary theatre's 'sensation drama', after which 'sensation novels' were named) is that of Hartright's meeting with Anne Catherick on the Finchley Road. Henry Dickens remembered his father's referring to the episode as one of the 'two scenes in literature which he regarded as being the most dramatic descriptions he could recall', the other being Carlyle's account in *The French Revolution* of the march of the women to Versailles. Remarking about some of the later scenes in *The Woman in White* that 'the excitement of the situation has a certain reality which makes the author's task easier', Margaret Oliphant shrewdly praised this scene and that of Hartright's dawning consciousness of a resemblance between Anne and Laura Fairlie as having a dramatic interest that was inward and psychological. As much as Carlyle, Collins captures a historical moment. Hartright has praised his late father's social orthodoxy. 'Thanks to his admirable prudence and self-denial my mother and sister were left, after his death, as independent of the world as they had been during his lifetime.' Prudence, self-denial, independence: these were the characteristic bourgeois virtues. While praising the characterisation of Marian and Count Fosco, admirers of *The Woman in White* have

often complained that Walter Hartright and Laura Fairlie are a
standard hero and heroine. The complaint is misconceived: the
hero and heroine are conventional; their characterisation is not.
There is a neat irony to the naming of Collins's hero. Hartright
sounds like a character in a morality play, and as such in mid-
nineteenth-century society was conventionally perceived. Those
with a right heart succeeded, while others failed. Hartright has to
adjust to the more complex social reality. By the late 1840s it was
becoming increasingly difficult to believe in the validity of the
moral ethic which was derived from *laissez-faire* economics, though
the ethic was preached all the more sternly in the face of doubt.
Laissez-faire capitalism recommended itself as tending towards
social equality: apart from inevitable cases of hardship which were
the province of charity and the Poor Laws, poverty was consequent upon the vices of individuals, who were intemperate,
imprudent or idle. Further, it was assumed that such poverty and
inequality as existed were more than adequately compensated by
the chances of rising in an open society. In the mid nineteenth
century, inequality was greater than ever before, within as well as
between classes, while the chances of rising socially were slight
and dwindling. Recommending self-help to the poor, remarks a
modern historian of the period, J. F. C. Harrison, was like telling
them to 'lift themselves up by their own bootstraps'.[6] Collins
shows a cynicism beginning to attach to the inculcation of
respectable values. In *The Woman in White*, Mrs Catherick is praised
for her 'independence of feeling' (p.154) in consigning at Sir
Percival Glyde's expense her daughter, Anne, to a private asylum.
Enunciating the principle that 'a truly wise Mouse is a truly good
Mouse' (p. 254), Fosco parodies the naïveté of Laura without being
himself more worldly wise than other contemporary moralists.

There is a real-life equivalent to the progress towards enlightenment of Hartright in *The Woman in White*. 'To Mr Collins', wrote
Henry James, 'belongs the credit of having introduced into fiction
those most mysterious of mysteries, the mysteries which are at our
own doors.' During the years in which *The Woman in White* is set,
Henry Mayhew was introducing readers of the *Morning Chronicle* to
mysteries at their own doors. Douglas Jerrold asked a correspon-
dent, Mrs Cowden Clarke, in 1850,

Do you devour those marvellous revelations of the inferno of
misery, of wretchedness, that is smouldering under our feet? We

live in a mockery of Christianity that, with the thought of its hypocrisy, makes us sick. We know nothing of this terrible life that is about us – us, in our smug respectability.

Writing contemporaneously with the first flowering of the domestic sagas, Mayhew shares in the creed of the literature. Introducing an account of the London costermongers, he remarked ruefully that 'the hearth, which is so sacred a symbol to all civilized races as being the spot where the virtues of each succeeding generation are taught and encouraged, has no charms to them'. Mayhew's report on the costermongers, however, showed that they spurned the hearth with impunity: although they rarely married, social chaos did not result and family and community life continued.[7] Mayhew came to appreciate that, so far from bad morals causing poverty, poverty caused the bad morals. Burlesquing the language of orthodoxy, he wrote of the casual dock-labourer's improvidence that it was

> due, therefore, not to any particular malformation of his moral constitution, but to the precarious character of his calling. His vices are the vices of ordinary human nature. . . . If the very winds could whistle away the food and firing of wife and children, I doubt much whether, after a week's or a month's privation, we should many of us be able to prevent ourselves from falling into the very same excesses.

In his novel set in the period of which Mayhew was conducting his researches, Collins, too, presented the moral invalids of conventional myth to his respectable audience ('we') as 'they' really were.

'This extraordinary apparition' (p. 47), Hartright calls Anne: she is dressed in white from head to foot. The conventional signification of female purity has in her case subversive implications. Apparitions abounded in Gothic fiction, the preceding literary sensationalism, and Collins often alludes to Gothic props to imply the contrasting realism and preoccupation with the present of his own sensation fiction. To Hartright, however, the unfortunate innocent whose existence orthodoxy denies must necessarily seem ghostly. Hartright simultaneously denies and conveys his reflex suspicion of Anne:

The one thing of which I felt certain was, that the grossest of
mankind could not have misconstrued her motive in speaking,
even at that suspiciously late hour and in that suspiciously
lonely place.   (p. 48)

Though one might assume that Hartright, in his capacity as
narrator, is expanding on momentary misgivings, these have
engrossed the time that they take to communicate, and the reader
in sympathy with Hartright is made a party to keeping Anne in
suspense. She has asked merely whether the road leads to London
and wonders whether Hartright heard her question. Aware of his
persisting mistrust, she protests her innocence:

You don't suspect me of doing anything wrong, do you? I have
done nothing wrong. I have met with an accident – I am very
unfortunate in being here alone so late. Why do you suspect me
of doing wrong?   (pp. 48–9)

Alert to Hartright's compulsion to associate misfortune with guilt,
Anne stresses the fortuity of her condition: she has 'met with an
accident'; she is 'very unfortunate'.
    Anne poses the crucial question: 'You don't think the worse of
me because I have met with an accident?' At this point, Hartright's
humanity would appear to have overriden his conditioning:

The natural impulse to assist her and to spare her got the better
of his judgement, the caution, the worldly tact, which an older,
wiser and colder man might have summoned to help him in this
strange emergency.   (p. 49)

The natural impulse takes Hartright only so far, and he continues
to prevaricate, instead of showing Anne where to find a cab. 'What
I did do, was to try and gain time by questioning her' (p. 50). The
aftermath of his eventual acquiescence is traumatic:

It was like a dream. Was I Walter Hartright? Was this the well-
known, uneventful road, where holiday people strolled on
Sundays? Had I really left, little more than an hour since, the
quiet, decent, conventionally-domestic atmosphere of my
mother's cottage?   (p. 50)

The conventionally domestic version of society, stressing the sufficiency of prudence and self-help, turns out to be the dream. Hartright is worried by 'a vague sense of something like self-reproach' (p. 51), without being able further to define this premonition of the immorality of conventional morality. He finds Anne a cab, but remains perplexed. The open conflict between benevolent impulse and the moral code in which he has been raised is still dreamlike:

> I hardly knew where I was going, or what I meant to do next; I was conscious of nothing but the confusion of my own thoughts, when I was abruptly recalled to myself – awakened, I might almost say – by the sound of rapidly approaching wheels close behind me. (p. 54)

Significantly, Hartright does not commit himself to the metaphor. He is 'awakened', almost, by the police, pursuing Anne at the instigation of Sir Percival Glyde. Hartright's confidence in the sweetness and light of the established form of society of which the police are guardians has been undermined.

Hartright, however, is yet the standard hero when he next meets Anne in Cumberland. Scrubbing the tomb of her late benefactress, Mrs Fairlie, Anne finds that convincing Hartright that her reputation is spotless is similarly hard work:

> It ought to be kept as white as snow, for her sake. I was tempted to begin cleaning it yesterday, and I can't help coming back to go on with it today. Is there anything wrong in that? I hope not. Surely nothing can be wrong that I do for Mrs Fairlie's sake?
>
> (p. 121)

Hartright's suspicions are as compulsive as Anne's scrubbing:

> Her 'misfortune'. In what sense was she using that word? In a sense which might explain her motive in writing the anonymous letter? In a sense which might show it to be the too common and too customary motive that has led many a woman to interpose anonymous hindrances to the marriage of the man who has ruined her? (p. 124)

Eventually in the novel, Hartright has no option but to extend in a manner which neither his own earlier self nor his father could have foreseen the principle of self-help. Having attributed to paranoia Anne Catherick's mistrust of 'men of rank and title' (p. 51), Hartright himself now senses a conspiracy of rank and power in England. Bent on hiding from his enemies the location of the lodgings which he shares with Laura and Marian in the East End of London, Hartright goes home by a lonely route to establish whether he is being followed:

> I had first learnt to use this stratagem against suspected treachery in the wilds of Central America – and now I was practising it again, with the same purpose and with even greater caution, in the heart of civilized London!   (p. 474)

If the wilds of Central America and civilised London seem curiously associated, so might civilised London and the Italy of the Risorgimento. Two Italian characters are prominent in the novel. Count Fosco combines his machinations against Laura with spying, on behalf of the Austrians who occupy his country, on fellow Italians in England. Walking from his house in St John's Wood, he stops by an Italian organ-grinder with his monkey. Mocking Mazzini's rhapsodic rhetoric, Fosco ignores the organ-grinder and presents a tart to the monkey. 'In the sacred name of humanity, I offer you some lunch!' (p. 587). The sensational plot culminates in 1851, the year, as Hartright remarks, 'of the famous Crystal Palace Exhibition' (p. 584). There are many foreigners in London. Fosco is attacked by Hartright through an Italian friend, Pesca, who found Hartright his appointment as drawing-master in Cumberland and still inescapably belongs to an Italian revolutionary society, 'the Brotherhood', which Fosco has betrayed. Pesca now regrets committing himself to revolution, but is yet prepared to defend his youthful decision:

> It is not for you to say – you Englishmen, who have conquered your freedom so long ago, that you have conveniently forgotten what blood you shed, and what extremities you proceeded to in the conquering – it is not for *you* to say how far the worst of all exasperations may, or may not, carry the maddened men of an enslaved nation.   (p. 595)

Besides being diminutive, Pesca is 'still further distinguished among the rank and file of mankind by the harmless eccentricity of his character' (p. 35). Recommending in *On Liberty* eccentricity as a good in itself, John Stuart Mill remarked that, 'precisely because the tyranny of opinion is such as to make eccentricity a reproach, it is desirable, in order to break through that tyranny, that people should be eccentric'. Pesca irritates Hartright's straitlaced sister by breaking a tea-cup. 'Very provoking: it spoils the Set' (p. 38). Paradoxically, Pesca's eccentricity is manifested in his emulating English respectability. He adopts athleticism and is to be seen 'invariably carrying an umbrella, and invariably wearing gaiters and a white hat' (p. 35). His Whiggish perspective on English history, which would imply that what the Italians were fighting for in the nineteenth century the English had won in the seventeenth, is not the last word in *The Woman in White* on the affinity between English and Italian history. If there were two nations in Italy, there might also be said to be, as Disraeli did say, two nations in England. Hartright follows the example of the Italian nationalists by taking the law into his own hands.

The action of *No Name*, Collins's next sensational novel, is dated with characteristic precision. The novel is set between the years 1846 and 1848. 1846 was the year of the significant middle-class triumph over aristocratic vested interests, the repeal of the Corn Laws. There is in Vauxhall Walk, where Noel Vanstone lives in Lambeth, a memorial of an aristocratic order which has vanished:

> And here – most striking object of all – on the site where thousands of lights once sparkled; where sweet sounds of music made night tuneful till morning dawned; where the beauty and fashion of London feasted and danced through the summer seasons of a century – spreads, at this day, an awful wilderness of mud and rubbish – the deserted dead body of Vauxhall Gardens mouldering in the open air. (p. 219)

If the revolutions of 1848 generally established the sway of the middle classes in the various countries, the 'June Days' in Paris, like Chartism in England, were a portent that the class which had triumphed might itself be eclipsed. The proletarian rising which began on 22 June 1848 in Paris was described by Marx as 'a gigantic insurrection, in which the first great battle was fought between the two great classes which divide modern society'. Those sceptical

whether Collins's dating will bear the significance being attributed
to it may be reminded that the eighteenth birthday of Rachel
Verinder in *The Moonstone* falls on 21 June 1848, and the moonstone
is removed in the early hours of the 22nd, a day which 'wore on to
its end drearily and miserably enough, I can tell you' (p. 218),
remarks Betteredge. In *No Name*, Collins described 'the hideous
London vagabond', lounging at the street-corners of Lambeth,

> the public disgrace of his country, the unheeded warning of
> social troubles that are yet to come. . . . Here, while the national
> prosperity feasts, like another Belshazzar, on the spectacle of its
> own magnificence, is the Writing on the Wall, which warns the
> monarch, Money, that his glory is weighed in the balance, and
> his power found wanting.   (p. 218)

In *No Name*, from within as well as without the dominant class, its
ideology is derided: Noel Vanstone, in the interview with his
disguised cousin, Magdalen, is bored by bourgeois moralism:
'Lecount, there, takes a high moral point of view – don't you,
Lecount? I do nothing of the sort. I have lived too long in the
continental atmosphere to trouble myself about moral points of
view.' He states his position, minus the moral dressing. 'I have got
the money, and I should be born idiot if I parted with it' (p. 242).
Noel's father, Michael Vanstone, has invoked providence in
defence of the same line of conduct. 'Let them understand that I
consider those circumstances to be a Providential interposition,
which has restored to me the inheritance that ought always to have
been mine' (p. 134). Michael Vanstone is a man of 1846, 'the
famous year' (p. 134), as Collins calls it, whose *Zeitgeist* is manifested in Andrew Vanstone's being killed in a railway accident.
Michael is a speculator, who does well out of the railway boom of
1846 without being caught in the subsequent crash: it is his
willingness to speculate on which Magdalen's plot to milk him of
his fortune is founded. It is a blow to Magdalen when her uncle
dies, since his son, Noel, a valetudinarian in his thirties, is bent
merely on maintaining intact his inherited capital. As a speculator,
who has been initially funded by his mother and a canny marriage,
Michael is no Smilesian hero, but, having made his fortune, he can
conceive of the rewards of his enterprise as a blessing. His son has
no incentive to take 'a high moral point of view' about money. Like
Mr Fairlie in *The Woman in White*, he is a character who signifies, in

the face of the moralists, the decreasing opportunities in mid-Victorian society of linking material well-being with any conceivable merit.

If Collins had been killed off by gout or laudanum in 1870, he might be more in repute today. Sensation novels, Margaret Oliphant suggested, were the characteristic literature of 'an age of events', the 1860s. The literary decline of Collins seems to be related at least as much the changed social climate in which he was writing in the 1870s as to gout, laudanum or the baneful influence of Reade. This is not to deny that personal factors were involved, but what should be stressed is the inadequacy of invoking gout to explain the peculiar social vision of the late fiction. One distressing feature of the later novels is the absence of irony. The basis of Collins's irony had been to play off the orthodoxy concerning social conventions, roles and institutions – that they were eternally and providentially ordained – against his own perception that they were historically relative and therefore transient. In *Man and Wife*, however, the present is represented, as Carlyle accused historians of representing the Reign of Terror, in hysterics. This particularly applies to the treatment of what from *Man and Wife* one might suppose, leaving aside the threat of unwary English tourists posed by the marriage laws in Scotland, to be the great social evil of the day, undergraduate athleticism. The athlete Geoffrey Delamayn has ideas 'of the devil's own'. 'A hideous cunning leered at his mouth and peeped out of his eyes' (p. 78). Collins claims that those who cultivate the body at the expense of the mind will be morally corrupted: Geoffrey Delamayn accordingly attempts to murder his wife. Collins also insists that physical cultivation is physically ruinous. Geoffrey fails to murder his wife because his athleticism induces a stroke. This is luridly described:

> Even as he raised the arm, a frightful distortion seized on his face. As if with an invisible hand, it dragged down the brow and the eyelid, on the right; it dragged down the mouth, on the same side. His arm fell helpless; his whole body, on the side under the arm, gave way. He dropped to the floor like a man shot dead.
>
> (p. 237)

Dr Benjulia, the heartless vivisectionist in *Heart and Science*, will commit suicide in his laboratory. Geoffrey has ignored urgent medical advice to stop running foot-races and his own death is a kind of suicide. Collins fictionally fulfils his own wishes, but actually he is paying tribute to what he senses is the durability of the present generation. 'The Rough with the clean skin and the good coat on his back', he remarks in the Preface to *Man and Wife*, 'is easily traced through the various grades of English society, in the middle and upper classes.' In the 1860s, these classes had seemed threatened from below. In the more placid atmosphere of the 1870s, Collins resorts to spontaneous combustion as the nemesis of the middle and upper classes.

Swinburne blamed the novelist's perdition on having missions. Paradoxically, the missionary impulse was linked to a newly pessimistic social perception. With the seemingly eternal middle-class back in apparent control of the wider world of facts, the words of George Eliot's Felix Holt seem oddly appropriate, for 'where great things can't happen I care [he tells us] for very small things'.

Royden Harrison has argued against the assimilation of the 1860s by historians of the Victorian period into an era of Victorian 'calm':

> In the 1860s the British working class exhibited certain 'contradictory' characteristics. If it was increasingly 'respectable', it was increasingly well organised. If it had abandoned its revolutionary ambitions, it had not wholly lost its revolutionary potentialities. It left no doubt that these potentialities might be speedily developed if it was too long thwarted in its desire to secure political equality. In short, it had attained precisely that level of development at which it was safe to concede its enfranchisement and dangerous to withhold it. It was this circumstance, rather than the death of Palmerston, which determined the timing of reform.[8]

The safety of the concession was not universally appreciated. The middle class imbued with the 'alarmed conservative feeling' detected by Matthew Arnold in 1866 was haunted no less by the spectre of what might amount to a legislative resolution than by that of violent revolution. Collins was a politically radical novelist, and George Eliot a very conservative one, but the shift in political attitude between the late 1860s and the early 1870s that is registered in her novels bears on the decline of Collins. In *Felix Holt the Radical*, published in 1866, Eliot is transparently nervous of the consequences of an extension of the franchise. Through her hero, she preaches the irrelevance of politics. To Felix Holt, as to Herbert Spencer, while men remain morally corrupt, corrupt statues will be corruptly administered. If men were not corrupt, there would be no need for legislation. The hysterical treatment of the Treby election riot, however, which is made to exemplify popular politics in action, implies that Eliot's deepest dread is not of politically motivated workers wasting their time. In 1868, after the Reform Act but before a reformed election, Eliot is still fraught. Felix Holt steps out of the novel into *Blackwood's Magazine* to address the workers, warning them, or pleading with them, neither to emulate the Fenians in Ireland nor to destroy the culture of which the rich are custodians. In *Middlemarch*, however, which appeared in four parts between 1871 and 1872, there is a placidity in Eliot's demonstration of the futility of Reform Acts. The brief appearances made in the novel by workers show them as less morally evolved but not exactly brutish.

Others, Engels included, were disappointed by the tranquil aftermath to the 1868 Reform Act. He wrote to Marx of the election that year that is was

a disastrous certificate of poverty for the English proletariat. . . . *The parson* has shown unexpected power, and so has the cringing to respectability. Not a single working-class candidate had a ghost of a chance, but my Lord Tumnoddy or any *parvenu* snob could have the workers' votes with pleasure.

The political headiness and surmise of the preceding years had been conducive to a minor renaissance of the historical novel, with Elizabeth Gaskell and Meredith treating the past both on its own terms and with a sense of the continuity between past and present which was reminiscent of Scott. By the end of the decade, historical novels had been superseded by historical romances such as *Lorna Doone*, which were announced as having no designs on the reader but to help him pass an idle hour. The major fiction of Collins must itself be seen as historical, notwithstanding that the history is recent. A sense of expanding options and possibilities in the future inspired the investigation into the past. By the early 1870s, that sense had vanished. The analogue in the fiction of Collins to the placidity of tone of *Middlemarch* is having missions. Both Eliot and Collins believe that 'great things can't happen'.

Notes

1. Elaine Showalter, *A Literature of their Own* (London: Virago, 1982) p. 162.
2. Ibid.
3. There is no standard edition of the work of Wilkie Collins. Editions cited are as follows: *The Woman in White* (Harmondsworth: Penguin, 1974); *The Moonstone* (Harmondsworth: Penguin, 1983); *Armadale* (London: Chatto and Windus, 1975); *No Name* (New York: Dover, 1983; *Man and Wife* (New York: Dover, 1983). Page references are given in brackets.
4. Sue Lonoff, *Wilkie Collins and his Victorian Readers* (New York: AMS Press, 1982) p. 1.
5. E. J. Hobsbawm, *The Age of Capital* (London: Sphere, 1977) p. 280.
6. J. F. C. Harrison, *The Early Victorians, 1832–51* (London: Fontana, 1973) p. 172. See also Harold Perkin, *The Origins of Modern English Society, 1780–1880* (London: Routledge and Kegan Paul, 1969) esp. ch. 10: 'Entrepreneurial Society: Ideal and Reality'.
7. Eileen Yeo makes this point in her essay, to which I am generally grateful, 'Mayhew as a Social Investigator', in E. P. Thompson and Eileen Yeo (eds), *The Unknown Mayhew* (Harmondsworth: Penguin, 1971).
8. Royden Harrison, *Before the Socialists* (London: Routledge and Kegan Paul, 1965) p. 133.

5

Sexual Politics and Political Repression in Bram Stoker's *Dracula*

ANNE CRANNY-FRANCIS

The characters and situations portrayed in Bram Stoker's *Dracula* provide fascinating insights into the social, political and psychological crises experienced by the middle classes in late-nineteenth-century Britain. *Dracula* is a compendium of the conflicting discourses which constituted bourgeois ideology in the late nineteenth century. Yet *Dracula* is not a socially critical text; rather it reproduces fictionally the contradictions within bourgeois ideology and then resolves or neutralises them. In this essay I have concentrated mainly on the ways in which Stoker's text responds to the challenge to patriarchal bourgeois society and ideology posed by the Women's Movement and the phenomenon of the 'New Woman'. I have considered the ways in which female characters are constituted in/by the text, and the kinds of situations in which the text places them and by which it asserts the (ideological) claims of male power and dominance. I have also considered briefly the characterisation of Dracula himself. The characterisation of the Count and the incidents in which he is involved may also be seen as dramatising some of the political and social dilemmas faced by the bourgeoisie in the late nineteenth century. First, however, it is necessary to establish how sexuality and sexual intercourse are signified in *Dracula*.

A number of the critical articles about *Dracula* are devoted to discovering and listing the kinds of sexual practices described or implied in the text. Christopher Bentley's 'The Monster in the Bedroom: Sexual Symbolism in Bram Stoker's *Dracula*' is masterful in this respect.[1] Necrophilia, incest, genital rape, oral rape, sadism, masochism, adultery, promiscuity, the evocation and violation of menstrual taboos, and castration are all detected by Bentley in 'symbolic' representation in *Dracula*. Writing of the 'baptism of blood' incident, which occurs late in the text and has Dracula forcing Mina to drink some of his own blood flowing from a self-imposed chest wound (p. 282),[2] Bentley notes,

> The episode contains a strange reversal of the usual relationship between vampire and victim, as Dracula is forcing Mina to drink his blood. Stoker is describing a symbolic act of enforced fellatio, where blood is again a substitute for semen, and where a chaste female suffers a violation that is essentially sexual.[3]

In fact it soon becomes apparent that, throughout the narrative, sexual intercourse is represented in displaced form as blood-sucking – so that, whereas in late-nineteenth-century British society 'normal' sexual behaviour was defined as male-initiated and male-dominant genital intercourse, in *Dracula* the practice which is the 'norm' and which gives all other (sexual) behaviour its meaning is male-initiated and male-dominant blood-sucking.

This does not mean that there are no female vampires in *Dracula*. The first encounter between vampire and victim in the text involves three female vampires. Soon after Harker discovers he is a prisoner in Dracula's castle, he explores some unused rooms looking for an escape route. Contrary to the Count's instructions, he falls asleep in one of the rooms. In a half-waking state he is approached by three young women, who have apparently ma-terialised out of thin air. Harker finds them almost irresistibly desirable and is about to succumb to their erotic advances 'in a languorous ecstasy' when the Count arrives. Dracula is enraged by the women's attempt to seduce Harker before he has given them permission, asserting, 'This man belongs to me!' The count then performs an act which is striking in its calculated repulsiveness. In response to the women's demands for 'food', he gives them a bag containing a baby, 'half smothered' but still alive (see pp. 36–9). The horror of this action is reinforced when, next day, the baby's mother arrives at the castle demanding her child's return. With the same callous indifference he had shown the child, Dracula sum-mons a wolf-pack which tears the woman to pieces (see p. 45).

These events and Harker's responses to them reveal a great deal about the attitude to women established in the text. Consider the latter incident, for example, when the woman is torn apart by the wolf-pack. Harker writes in his diary, 'I could not pity her, for I knew now what had become of her child, and she was better dead' (p. 45). It is clear from this entry that, at least as far as Harker is concerned (and Harker is the sympathetic hero of the novel), the main value of women lies in their maternal function. Having lost the ability to perform this function, through loss of her child, it is only fitting that the woman be destroyed (note that no similar conclusion is drawn about Godalming's future after Lucy's death). Even more significant, however, is the response to the vampire women elicited by this episode. They appear absolutely monstrous.

Dracula's act in taking the child is bad enough, but can be somehow understood in terms of the Count's declared mastery over the peasants of the region. The women's action in using the baby as food has no such justification. Its horror is largely a function of the role-reversal acted out in the situation. The women, instead of providing nourishment for the baby from their own bodies in the traditional female maternal role, actually incorporate the baby as well as its blood into their own bodies as nourishment. Yet the significance of this incident for the portrayal of the vampire women does not stop here. Recall the initial premise, that bloodsucking is to be read in the text as sexual intercourse. The violence committed by the women on the baby is, by implication, not only physical; it is also sexual. They are not only homicidal maniacs; they are also child-molesters. It is useful now to consider the effect of the juxtaposition in the narrative of this baby-stealing episode with the attempted seduction of Harker.

By their attack on the baby the three women are coded as not just abnormally aggressive or violent, but as abnormally sexually aggressive. Their approach to Harker is to be read in the same way, as abnormally sexually aggressive. The assumption underlying this sequence of significances is that normal women – women who accept their proper role as mothers – are passive and sexually receptive, not initiatory. The titillation value of these women in the text is precisely a function of their transgression of conventional behaviour, a transgression which will, inevitably, be punished.

An interesting aspect of Harker's response to the female vampires (and note that the term 'vampire', with its connotations of sexual aggressiveness, is so conventionally male that the gender adjective has to be used to identify the women, but never Dracula) is his feeling that he knows one of them:

The other was fair, as fair as can be, with great, wavy masses of golden hair and eyes like pale sapphires. I seemed somehow to know her face, and to know it in connection with some dreamy fear, but I could not recollect at the moment how or where.

(p. 37)

Phyllis Roth, in her article 'Suddenly Sexual Women in Bram Stoker's *Dracula*',[4] suggests that the face Harker recognises is that of the mother, 'she whom he desires yet fears, the temptress–seductress, Medusa', and that 'this golden girl reappears in the early description of Lucy'.[5] Roth's identification of this implied correspondence between Lucy and the female vampire is crucial to an understanding of the dynamics of the narrative. Just as Milton damned Eve long before the arrival of the serpent in *Paradise Lost* by means of the terms used to describe her – terms which suggest her collusion with the forces of evil, the serpent – so Stoker uses the suggestion of a likeness between Lucy and the vampire to prepare readers not only to accept her fate, but also to see it as somehow justified. Harker's almost-recognition of the vampire as Lucy introduces the notion that there is some essential similarity between the two. That similarity is sexual assertiveness or aggression.

The reader is introduced to Lucy through a series of letters she exchanges with Mina Murray, Harker's fiancée. Lucy's first letters concern her recent engagement to Arthur Holmwood (Lord Godalming) and her distress at having to disappoint her other two suitors, Dr John Seward, a psychiatrist, and Quincey P. Morris, an American millionaire. In her second letter she writes, 'Why can't they let a girl marry three men, or as many as want her, and save all this trouble? But this is heresy, and I must not say it' (p. 59). Of course she has said it, and many commentators have noted that this is an unconventionally candid, almost risqué, statement. Yet it is not difficult to discover Stoker's motives in ascribing this speech to Lucy. Like her resemblance to the female vampire it signifies the sensuality which characterises Lucy as a vampire. What she later becomes – a sexually aggressive (and therefore 'abnormal') woman – is seen as implicit in her behaviour even before Dracula arrives in England. Lucy's sexual aggressiveness – displaced as the vampire's bloodlust – will be seen as her greatest crime and will provoke a combined male assault and assertion of dominance.

When the reader is first introduced to Lucy, however, there is no suggestion that she actually is sexually active or unusually sexually aware. Rather the reader is told of Lucy's great beauty and sweetness, which make her an object of desire for the men with whom she comes in contact. Mina notes that even the old, retired sailors at Whitby 'did not lose any time in coming up and sitting near her when we sat down. She is so sweet with old people; I think they all fell in love with her on the spot' (p. 64). And it is this beauty, this blatant signifier of Lucy's female sexuality, which is her only crime. The guilt experienced by men as a result of their desire is displaced onto the woman who stimulates that desire; she is seen as the source of immorality, of sensuality, while they are not. If she is destroyed, they will be saved. It is a familiar story, and it is acted out again in *Dracula*.

The scene in which Lucy is killed is one of the most brutal and repulsive in the book. Lucy's beauty has already apparently stung the vampire to desire, and she becomes his first English (rape) victim. Yet it is she who suffers for this, by becoming an Undead – loathsome in the sight of man (!) and God. Her sensual appearance as a vampire is a kind of perverse apotheosis of her female sexuality and it is brutally, sadistically destroyed by her male companions – the very men to whom she is/was so attractive. Once her body has been pierced and mutilated by the men, Lucy's face regains its 'unequalled sweetness and purity' (pp. 216–17). In other words, the sexual initiative is restored to the men and patriarchy is reassured by the negation of Lucy's 'aggressive' (because apparent) female sexuality. She can henceforth live on as a beautiful, spiritual memory for all of them – her troublesome physical presence removed.

The analogy between Lucy and the female vampires at Dracula's castle is made explicit when it is revealed that Lucy's early vampire attacks are all on children. The same sequence of significations then operates, and Lucy's behaviour is seen as abominable.

Lucy's role in the narrative supports the thesis already put forward: that in *Dracula* Stoker acts out the threat posed by women to the patriarchal society of the late nineteenth century – either by sexually aggressive women whom he refuses to identify as female, or by beautiful women whose sexuality is aggressive only in that men find it impossible to ignore.

Further evidence that the female vampires are to be read as abnormally sexually aggressive occurs in Harker's final journal entry before his escape from the castle. The identification of female sexuality as naturally passive and receptive is again apparent in Harker's refusal to accept that the female vampires are women: 'I am alone in the castle with those awful women. Faugh! Mina is a woman, and there is naught in common. They are devils of the Pit!' (p. 53). Harker's desperation to escape from the castle is a transparent fear of castration. What he fears is not death, but the loss of sexual initiative and dominance which for him (and those who accept patriarchal values) means the loss of his male sexuality: 'At least God's mercy is better than that of these monsters, and the precipice is steep and high. At its foot man may sleep – as a man' (p. 53).

This passage, along with Harker's near-recall of Lucy, sets up an opposition which has an important structuring function in the narrative: Mina/Lucy. By means of this opposition Stoker constructs the conventional – and contradictory – definition of women. They are simultaneously sexually aggressive and tempting, and sexually passive and receptive. Lucy and the female vampires represent the alluring (in both senses of the word) woman who is present in all women and must be destroyed if patriarchy is to be maintained (and, of course, the fun – titillation – of patriarchy is this assertion of male dominance, the taming/destruction of the female). Mina, on the other hand, represents the sexually passive, submissive woman – though, interestingly, she is also described as highly intelligent. In fact, the characterisation of Mina is more complex than that of Lucy in that it represents the convergence of conflicting discourses, traditional and 'New' woman.

Stoker introduces the notion of the 'New Woman' several times in *Dracula*. After Mina and Lucy have had tea at a Whitby inn, Mina records in her journal, 'I believe we should have shocked the "New Woman" with our appetites. Men are more tolerant, bless them!' (p. 88). Later in the same entry she disapprovingly notes,

> Some of the 'New Woman' writers will some day start an idea that men and women should be allowed to see each other asleep before proposing or accepting. But I suppose the New Woman won't condescend in future to accept; she will do the proposing herself. (p. 89)

Stoker, it seems, introduces the 'New Woman' idea in order to dissociate his heroines from the Women's Movement. Nevertheless, some critics have argued that, in Mina, Stoker is describing one of the New Women; that Stoker strongly supported female emancipation, and that *Dracula* provides examples of strong female characterisation. Proof of this is held to be Mina's resourcefulness in using a typewriter and negotiating and memorising railway timetables (railways then signifying technological sophistication), as well as her efficient and logical note-taking and her intelligent contributions to discussions concerning the Count. This efficiency and clear-thinking earn her a very high compliment; she is said to think like a man. Van Helsing himself offers this praise: 'Ah, that wonderful Madam Mina! She has man's brain – a brain that a man should have were he so gifted – and woman's heart' (p. 234).

Through the role of Lucy in the narrative Stoker has shown how any transgression of traditional sexual roles, intentional or not, will be treated. The reader would now be justified in asking how Mina's appropriation of the male prerogatives of intelligence and efficiency can be tolerated. Stoker resolves this apparent contradiction – Mina's unfemale/unfeminine intelligence – on several levels. First, it must be remembered that Mina has been granted this accolade by a man, Van Helsing, and that he defines it as a male attribute. So men are still seen as dominating and controlling the agency by which women are recognised as intelligent; a woman is intelligent if or because men think she thinks like them. In this sense, then, Mina's New Woman qualifications are highly suspect. More important and disturbing, however, is the disposition of Mina's body and sexuality in the narrative.

Critical commonplaces in the study of *Dracula* are that Mina is less sexually threatening than Lucy and that this is the reason she is eventually saved. Also Mina adopts the conventional (and, as we have seen, approved) female role of the mother several times in the text. She offers motherly comfort to Lord Godalming after Lucy's death:

> We women have something of the mother in us that makes us rise above smaller matters when the mother-spirit is invoked; I felt this big, sorrowing man's head resting on me, as though it were that of the baby that some day might lie on my bosom, and I stroked his hair as though he were my own child.   (p. 230)

And, at the end of the novel, in a final journal entry by Harker, the reader learns that Mina has had a baby boy: 'His bundle of names links all our little band of men together; but we call him Quincey' (p. 378).

It has also been noted that no heterosexual sex is depicted, even suggested, in the book, and that it comes to seem almost unthinkable to the reader that Jonathan and Mina should have any kind of sexual relationship. Given the chain of significances established in the narrative, the displacement of genital heterosexuality as blood-sucking, this is not surprising. Within this narrative, genital heterosexuality is considerably displaced from the 'norm' and would therefore seem extremely perverse. Nevertheless, Harker's sexuality is given expression in the narrative, in his rejection of the sexually aggressive female vampires and his efforts to protect his (properly maternal) wife from the vampire. Mina's sexuality, on the other hand, has no expression; it is completely muted, neutered.

We have already seen that Mina is characterised by her 'masculine' intelligence and her maternal, nurturing temperament, both of which deflect attention from her female sexuality. Also Mina does not have Lucy's great beauty and so does not provoke desire in the men around her. She is, therefore, perceived as innocent, guiltless, and almost childishly asexual. Then she is attacked by the vampire – and her sexuality, so effectively (!) concealed by intelligence and motherliness, is made apparent. And it is made apparent in the most shocking way – in the 'baptism of blood' incident discussed at the beginning of this essay. The (displaced) oral rape is followed by the beginning of Mina's metamorphosis – into a sexually assertive, sensual woman – and this the men cannot allow. Mina is eventually saved (i.e. destroyed) because she colludes with the men, accepting her rape as a sign of her own guilt: 'Unclean! unclean! I must touch him or kiss him (her husband) no more' (p. 254); 'Unclean! Unclean! Even the almighty shuns my polluted flesh!' (p. 296). Mina's assertion of her own guilt means that the men do not have to identify this relationship (though Van Helsing comes close), and patriarchy is once again saved from its own deconstruction. Following this incident in the narrative Mina submits herself entirely to the control of the men, voluntarily excluding herself from the conferences held to plan the attack on Dracula. With her sexuality aroused, her intelligence can no longer be trusted. In fact, only when she is hypnotised by Van Helsing are her thoughts and perceptions regarded as reliable. In a consummate act of submission Mina asks that, in the event that Dracula does gain mastery over her, the men should kill her:

> Then I shall tell you plainly what I want, for there must be no doubtful matter in this connection between us now. You must promise me, one and all – even you, my beloved husband – that, should the time come, you will kill me.   (p. 330)

In her acceptance of patriarchal ideology Mina asks that, if she transgresses patriarchal norms by becoming sexually assertive, the men should return her to normality – rendering her sexually passive, submissive, receptive.

As noted earlier, the characterisation of Mina has been seen as a site of conflicting discourses. Her technical skill and efficiency and her intelligence identify her as a 'New Woman', while her sexual passivity, her motherliness and submissiveness mark her as a traditional woman. Some critics therefore see Mina as an amalgam of old and new, the woman who survives the ordeals (of conflicting social pressures) and will go on to produce a new and enlightened society.[6] But skill, efficiency and intelligence are specifically identified with the 'New Woman' only by those who accept traditional values (whether Stoker and/or his readers), believing that women are technically incompetent and stupid.[7] It is surely more to the point to note that the attributes given to Mina which suggest power, ability, assertiveness are progressively appropriated by the men around her. Her intelligence is seen as a masculine attribute to which she has somehow gained access – it is not naturally available to women; while the potential threat of the intelligent woman is averted by a display of male physical, intellectual and sexual dominance and of female submission. There is nothing in the text to suggest any kind of belief in the 'New Woman'. There are gestures which identify aspects of the contemporary feminist movement, such as the demands that women's sexual needs and intelligence be recognised. These demands were interpreted as violent attacks on the conventional female social role. In *Dracula* these demands are dramatised, their transgressiveness is revealed, and they are then rejected. Rather than championing women's rights or a revaluation of traditional female roles, *Dracula* enacts the male-dominated (patriarchal) suppression of any violation of those roles. When these violations are described in the narrative, they may have a titillatory appeal. But they are titillatory *because* they are circumscribed within a male-dominated ideology which can, apparently at will, devalue and/or destroy them.

In *The Literature of Terror* David Punter writes of this function of Gothic literature,

> Gothic enacts psychological and social dilemmas: in doing so, it both confronts the bourgeoisie with its limitations and offers it modes of imaginary transcendence, which is after all the dialectical role of most art. Gothic fiction demonstrates the *potential* of revolution by daring to speak the socially unspeakable; but the very act of speaking it is an ambiguous gesture.[8]

In *Dracula* the dilemma created by growing demands for female emancipation is acted out. However, the dilemma is not that of women – and men – trapped in unpleasant, repressive social roles. It is the dilemma of a male-dominated bourgeoisie unwilling to change, or even seriously examine, behaviour patterns/social roles which are seen as fundamental to the operation of the British (capitalist) social and economic system. For them any challenge to traditional male and female social roles was an attack on the system itself. In *Dracula* these fears are vicariously acted out and then banished. The potentially revolutionary attributes of the female characters – sexual candour and intelligence - are destroyed, one way or another. The sexual candour is punished by sexual means, by a kind of gang rape, which crudely asserts masculine strength and power. Mina's intelligence is undermined first by being nominated masculine and then by the negation of Mina's female sexuality. Mina is bereft of any female intelligence, since by definition it does not exist. She is defined as a woman not by her sexuality and, therefore, worrying desirability, but by her maternity and maternal nature. The sexually aggressive woman is destroyed, rendered passive, negated, so that she can no longer threaten men. The intelligent woman has her sexuality negated, her body subdued to the wishes and directions of men, and her intelligence appropriated by men as a specifically masculine mode of thought. For those who accepted the patriarchal ideology of the late nineteenth century, *Dracula* provided a way of dealing vicariously with the anxieties aroused by ideas and movements which were calling into doubt the justice and consistency of that ideology.

As noted above, the attack on sexual roles was also interpreted more widely as an attack on the capitalist economic system itself; sexual anxiety was compounded with political fears by the bourgeoisie. *Dracula* can also be seen as expressing some of the political fears of the middle classes. Linda Dowling's article 'The Decadent and the New Woman in the 1890s'[9] is a fascinating exploration of the perceived relationship between decadent dandy or homosexual and the socially aware, politicised woman in the late nineteenth century. The decadent and the New Woman were seen as sharing several attributes. For example, both were in favour of non-reproductive sex; the dandy often as a result of sexual preference, the New Woman because she insisted on women's right to contraceptive information as a means of controlling their own bodies. This was commonly seen as a rejection of the family and a potential cause of the breakdown – if not extinction – of society. Dowling records the response of *Punch* to these new phenomena:

> *Punch* devoted a good deal of space to the eugenic dangers raised by contemporary male effeminacy and female manishness; the New Woman 'made further development in generations to come quite impossible' (21 July 1894, p. 27) while the 'New Man' was, in a word, 'Woman' (24 November 1894, p. 249).[10]

Both decadent and New Woman were regarded as significant political threats to bourgeois capitalist society, their non-conformity signifying 'cultural anarchism and decay'.[11] In *Dracula* Stoker presents the quintessence of non-reproductive sex, the blood-sucking of the vampire. Yet, in a perverse way, the vampire does reproduce, transforming her/his victim into a vampire; in the place of non-reproductive sex Stoker substitutes non-sexual reproduction. The threatened result is a society of non-productive, parasitic, culturally anarchic beings whose will is subordinated to the will of the primogenitor, Dracula. Though this projection is not made in the text, its inconsistency with bourgeois ideology is all too apparent. We have already seen how, in *Dracula*, one aspect of the political challenge to bourgeois ideology is confronted and resolved. Other analyses of the political function of the text concentrate on the characterisation of the Count himself, product of Gothic at a time 'exemplified particularly in Wilde and in Bram Stoker, when decadence, engaged in picking over the bones of aristocratic modes of life, starts to travel again in vampiristic circles'.[12]

Richard Wasson, in 'The Politics of *Dracula*',[13] and David Punter in *The Literature of Terror*, both concentrate on the characterisation of Dracula. Punter notes the significance of Dracula's noble ancestry to a bourgeoisie fascinated by the unattainable prestige and power of noble 'blood'. The Count is a vestige of feudalism in a thoroughly capitalised, capitalist country. As Dracula tells Harker before his departure for London,

> Here I am noble; I am *boyar*; the common people know me, and I am master. But a stranger in a strange land, he is no one.... I have been so long master that I would be master still – or at least that none should be master of me.   (p. 20)

In the bourgeois society of the late nineteenth century Dracula is an alien, an irritation and a potential threat. Punter notes the chain of oppositions set up in the text by his characterisation:

> Dracula stands for lineage, the principal group of characters for family; Dracula for the wildness of night, they for the security of day; Dracula for unintelligible and bitter passion, they for the sweet and reasonable emotions; Dracula for the physical and erotic, they for repressed and etherealised love.[14]

Further, Dracula stands for the mysterious, magical East, they for the rational, technologised West; Dracula for the alien, they for the domestic. In ways discussed by Wasson and Punter, the story of Dracula – like that of the female characters – enacts social and psychological crises of late-nineteenth-century British capitalist society.

About the time *Dracula* was written, Britain was just starting to emerge from what economic historians call the 'Great Depression' which lasted from 1873 to 1896. During this period, as Eric Hobsbawm records in *Industry and Empire*, Britain 'ceased to be the "workshop of the world" and became merely one of its three greatest industrial powers; and, in some crucial respects, the weakest of them'.[15] With smaller, growing economies using tariff and protection to nurture their fledgling industry, Britain had only one way out of its economic problems – imperialism. Hobsbawm notes that, although imperialism was not new to Britain, the loss of its imperialist monopoly was:

> What was new was the end of the virtual British monopoly on the underdeveloped world, and the consequent necessity to mark out regions of imperial influence formally against potential competitors; often ahead of any actual prospects of economic benefits; often, it must be admitted, with disappointing economic results.[16]

On the domestic scene, the years from the mid-1870s to mid-1890s saw the emergence of mass working-class political movements in countries throughout Europe. Capitalist society in the mid-1890s was clearly in a state of dilemma, if not crisis. These economic and political factors generated their own social and psychological consequences: jingoism and xenophobia, resulting from the need to colonise and the competition for imperialist plunder; insecurity and class-hatred, bred by fear of the growing political power of the working classes; cultural insecurity, engendered by the bourgeois sensitivity to the manufacturing background of their wealth, in contrast to the 'nobility' of the aristocratic landlord; disillusionment and despair, bred by the progressive replacement of traditional faiths and beliefs by the positivist discourse of this scientifically and technologically advanced society. The pursuit and destruction of the vampire can be seen as acting out a number of these anxieties, in order to contain them – in much the same way as the destruction of the female characters can be seen as exorcising the threat of the Women's Movement.

As an ancient, East European aristocrat, Dracula characterises many of the conflicts facing the late-nineteenth-century bourgeois. As an aristocrat (the multiple signification of the 'blood' in the text is surely not accidental) Dracula recalls the vestiges of feudal ideology which continued to exist in conflict with the contemporary capitalist ideological discourse. His dominating presence and assumption of mastery, which are a function of his nobility, signify the sort of individualism to which bourgeois ideologists obsessively laid claim, but consistently failed to produce or achieve. In his individualism Dracula represented the kind of anarchic political force associated with the New Woman, decadent, and the working classes. Like them he refused to be bound by bourgeois ideology and bourgeois values. So, like these other anti-bourgeois forces, Dracula has to be destroyed.

Dracula's extreme age and Eastern origin also identify him with another problematic situation faced by the middle classes – described by Richard Wasson:

> These themes add up to the idea that technological progress, having cut humanity off from the old superstitious, dark knowledge, makes itself increasingly vulnerable to the demonic powers like the Vampire, for, having written them off as unreal, civilized man has no defense against them. Since only doctors of the mind, Seward and Van Helsing, can cope with such monsters the novel carries the implication that demonish forces have been unloosed in the human psyche by technological and political progress.[17]

Interestingly, Van Helsing and Seward do not deal with the threat of the demonish/non-conformist/non-bourgeois simply by means of modern technology. They use technology in association with a ritualistic, superstitious manipulation not of religion, but of religious symbols, such as the host and the cross. What the interaction between Dracula and the men enacts is the clash of conflicting discourses which problematises bourgeois ideology: the positivist discourse of technology and the new 'scientific' world view and the Christian discourse which, nominally at least, governed the ethical and moral practices of that society. If the positivist discourse is to emerge dominant, then the religious discourse must be subordinated, as it is in this narrative where it retains only its emotional and psychological effects. As Wasson writes in another context, 'modern victories can be better won by subversion'.[18]

Many other significances have been detected in the struggle between Dracula and the men, involving Dracula's identity as alien, as father, as anti-Christ. As in the episodes discussed above, the interactions between Dracula and the men usually enact situations of social and psychological crisis within bourgeois ideology, resolving vicariously the contradictions which problematise bourgeois ideology. Rosemary Jackson writes of Stoker's work and of Gothic fantasy in general,

> Very clearly with *The Lair of the White Worm*, but equally so with *Dracula*, Stoker reinforces social, class, racial and sexual pre-

judices. His fantasies betray the same tendency as many
Victorian texts: they manipulate apparently non-political issues
into forms which would serve the dominant ideology.... The
shadow on the edges of bourgeois culture is variously identified,
as black, mad, primitive, criminal, socially deprived, deviant,
crippled, or (when sexually assertive) female.... Through this
identification, troublesome social elements can be destroyed in
the name of exorcising the demonic. Many fantasies play upon a
natural fear of formlessness, absence, 'death', to reinforce an
apparently 'natural' order of life – but that order is in effect an
arbitrary one which identified the 'norm' as a middle-class,
monogamous and male-dominated culture. In the name of
defeating the 'inhuman' such fantasies attempt to dismiss forces
inimical to a bourgeois ideology.[19]

In this essay I have looked particularly at the constitution of
female sexuality in *Dracula* and at how the book enacts and
resolves the crisis produced within bourgeois ideology by the
emergence of the emancipation movement, which revealed the
contradictory and unjust treatment of women within that ideology.
I have also looked briefly at some of the situations involving
Dracula and at the characterisation of the Count. And again
Stoker's text can be seen as fulfilling an ideologically conservative
role, acting out other problematic situations in order to resolve
contradictions revealed in bourgeois ideology. Perhaps the most
interesting aspect of the critical analysis of a book like *Dracula* is
discovering how these mechanisms of resolution and repression
operate. David Punter notes of Gothic that 'it actually demonstrates within itself the mechanisms which enforce non-fulfil-
ment'.[20] In Bram Stoker's *Dracula* one manifestation of the socially/
psychologically/politically repressive apparatus of late-nineteenth-
century British bourgeois ideology can be seen in action: no
wonder Dracula felt like a 'stranger in a strange land'.

Notes

1. C. F. Bentley, 'The Monster in the Bedroom: Sexual Symbolism in Bram Stoker's *Dracula'*, *Literature and Psychology*, 22 (1972) 27–34.
2. Page references relate to Bram Stoker, *Dracula*, with an introduction and notes by A. N. Wilson (Oxford: Oxford University Press, 1983). Quotations from the novel are from this edition.
3. Bentley, in *Literature and Psychology*, 22, p. 30.
4. Phyllis A. Roth, 'Suddenly Sexual Woman in Bram Stoker's *Dracula'*, *Literature and Psychology*, 26 (1977) 113–21.
5. Ibid., p. 119.
6. See, for example, Carol A. Senf, *'Dracula*: Stoker's Response to the New Woman', *Victorian Studies*, 26, no. 1 (Autumn 1982) 33–49.
7. Certainly some readers were aware that this kind of identification referred not to women's actual abilities, but to the social representation of their abilities. In Stoker's text, however, I can find no evidence that this distinction has been made.
8. David Punter, *The Literature of Terror: A History of Gothic Fictions from 1765 to the Present Day* (London: Longman, 1980) p. 417.
9. Linda Dowling, 'The Decadent and the New Woman in the 1890s', *Nineteenth-Century Fiction*, 33 (1979) 434–53.
10. Ibid., p. 445.
11. Ibid., p. 440.
12. Punter, *The Literature of Terror*, pp. 206–7.
13. Richard Wasson, 'The Politics of *Dracula'*, *English Literature in Transition*, 9 (1966) 24–7.
14. Punter, *The Literature of Terror*, p. 259.
15. E. J. Hobsbaum, *Industry and Empire: From 1750 to the Present Day*, in *The Pelican Economic History of Britain*, III (Harmondsworth: Pelican, 1969) 104.
16. Ibid., p. 107.
17. Wasson, in *English Literature in Transition*, 9, p. 25.
18. Ibid., p. 25.
19. Rosemary Jackson, *Fantasy: The Literature of Subversion* (London: Methuen, 1981) pp. 121–2.
20. Punter, *The Literature of Terror*, p. 409.

6

The Vampire in the Looking-Glass: Reflection and Projection in Bram Stoker's *Dracula*

PHILIP MARTIN

The history of *Dracula*'s reception is a history composed of a series of usurpations. As the reproductions and revisions of the cinema have usurped the original text, so too the original text has usurped its author. While *Dracula* survives and continues as a living myth of popular fiction, Bram Stoker has passed away into relative obscurity. The peculiar survival of his text as a classic of a kind owes very little to the abiding interests and concerns of the literary or academic establishments, and its presence in our culture does not directly derive from an evaluation of its author's skills. In this sense, some may regard it as a peculiarly 'pure' text, comparatively free from critical attention, and fortunately bereft of the stigmata commonly induced in texts burdened with concepts of authorial genius. This notion might be developed into a declaration of *Dracula* as a beautifully clean text, a classic that has not been manufactured, but one that has survived through its self-per-petuating mythic appeal.[1] There may be a partial truth in such an idea, but it is dangerously idealistic, for such a formula takes no account of the social conditions or cultural politics that have governed *Dracula*'s success. Those conditions, broadly, are the conditions of the cinema, and the salability of anxiety (for *Dracula* is rarely a horror film in the fullest sense). Few people come to the text having never seen a screen production of some kind, so, while the book remains free from critical molestation, it is still subject to a corresponding process of mediation, as it is commonly read with a number of associations deriving from at least one of the many films. The conditions of cinema reproduction in which I am more interested, however, are the conditions described by Pirandello and endorsed by Walter Benjamin.[2]

In a comparison between the stage actor and the screen actor, Pirandello noted how the latter, bereft of an immediate audience, suffers alienation 'from the stage and from himself' in a production which sells the camera-manufactured personality which is not his own.[3] The emptiness which Pirandello and Benjamin describe finds a startling coincidence in the role which the representation of the figure of Dracula himself demands:

> With a vague sense of discomfort he feels inexplicable emptiness: his body loses its corporeality, it evaporates, it is deprived of reality, life, voice, and the noises caused by his moving about, in order to be changed into a mute image, flickering an instant on the screen, then vanishing into silence. . . .[4]

This is most clearly manifested in Murnau's seminal silent version of 1922. Yet many of the screen versions of *Dracula*, knowingly or otherwise, have exploited this peculiar coincidence between Bram Stoker's discomfited Romantic hero and the acting which his role demands, and nowhere is this more acutely or oddly felt than in the scene where Dracula's image is not reflected in the mirror. For this is also the overbearing strangeness described by Benjamin as being akin to 'the estrangement felt before one's image in the mirror'.[5] The alienation of the film actor before the camera is the emptiness of Dracula himself, who may not enter the world of the living and the dead. Both stare into a mirror/lens that will not permit their passage to the worlds they represent. Beyond them, therefore, is the conspiracy between the world of scientific normality inside and outside the film itself: Van Helsing's mirror is the ultimate test debarring Dracula access to his world, and his trust in his optic device corresponds almost quaintly with the good faith that the audience maintain in the more sophisticated optical apparatus of camera, projector and cellulose. So Dracula's presence in our culture depends largely upon the constant reiteration of his exclusion. He is an impossibility: subjected to the scrutiny of the lens and the mirror, he is condemned to remain outside in perpetual exile.

This impossibility has a correspondence within the text itself, whose various narratives hover uncertainly around Dracula and his vampires, frequently supplying more than one account of the same incident as they attempt to explain in language what language will not allow. Consequently, we only ever receive from the book's narrators the projections decreed by their linguistic knowledge, which in some cases (Mina's shorthand, for instance) is retranscribed. In Harker's words, 'there is hardly one authentic document!' p. 499).[6] The authenticity of the events upon the cinema screen relies on a total dependence on the reliability of the camera (which is, and yet is not, the mirror), but the authenticity of the text is less certain, more rich in ambiguity, since it depends upon the reader's acceptance of the language codes which the narrators employ.

I shall take Van Helsing's mirror (or Harker's, or Mina's – depending which 'text' is followed) as being of central symbolic importance. It is very close to the mirror of Lacan. It represents the test of the socially 'normal' world which the characters in the book represent, for the recognition of the self in the mirror is the recognition of the otherness of being, the early step towards socialisation.[7] Dracula cannot perceive this otherness, nor, in Bram Stoker's text, can anyone else see it for him. (In the films by Murnau and Herzog, however, Mina – here called Lucy – is granted this perception, and consequently saves the Count by recognising him fully as her lover.) He is never able to see himself as a being operating within a social world of otherness which demands the repression of infantile fantasies of omnipotent power. This power he retains and exploits: he never moves through the mirror stage to accept the 'reality' of the world constructed through language. And just as he, on the one side, shows no understanding of the norms of that world, so, on the other, the narrators use the very language which *excludes* Dracula as their only means of describing him. The task that faces the reader is the examination of this slippage, the gulf between the narratives and what they unwittingly recognise as Dracula's significance.

It is the central symbolic ritual – the taking of blood – which deserves the weight of our consideration, for it is that which the narrators' language struggles with. The terms used combine in an uncomfortable equation of moral condemnation, bodily disgust and the pleasures of sexual desire, and they remain unreconciled in all cases. In the first of these rituals (which is incomplete) Jonathan Harker finds a new pleasure in discovering that his conventional role as dominant partner has been usurped:

All three had brilliant white teeth, that shone like pearls against the ruby of their voluptuous lips. There was something about them that made me uneasy, some longing and at the same time some deadly fear. I felt in my heart a wicked burning desire that they would kiss me with those red lips.   (p. 51)

The *frisson* of anticipation is heightened, here as elsewhere, through the confessional nature of the writing: Harker's journal itself is a means whereby the pleasures and pains of his experience may be relived. He lies, he tells us, in 'an agony of delightful anticipation' in a mixture of pleasure and fear 'both thrilling and repulsive' (pp. 51–2). The scene is a thinly disguised representation of the desire for the woman and the fear of the woman: the desire for sexual fulfilment and the fear of its enervating consequences which find a symbolic articulation in Harker's fear that he will become 'a banquet ... to those horried three' (p. 67). This is further developed as Harker smells the breath of the first vampire, which he describes as 'sweet ... in one sense, honey-sweet ... but with a bitter underlying the sweet, a bitter offensiveness, as one smells in blood!' (p. 52). The conflation is too obvious to pass without comment. It expresses the attractions of the vagina and the fear of its blood, the inability of Harker (to use Freud's words) to 'dissociate the puzzling phenomenon of this monthly flow of blood from sadistic ideas' and, of course, from the fantasies of castration that attend it.[8]

This first vampiric ceremony sets the broad pattern for those which follow. It is exorcised by the all-powerful male, in this instance Dracula himself, whose power is magnified by reference to the strength of the woman he overthrows:

I saw his strong hand grasp the slender neck of the fair woman and with giant's power draw it back, the blue eyes transformed with fury, the white teeth champing with rage, and the fair cheeks blazing red with passion. But the Count! Never did I imagine such wrath and fury, even in the demons of the pit. . . . With a fierce sweep of his arm, he hurled the woman from him, and then motioned to the others, as though he were beating them back . . . .   (p. 53)

The restitution of the man's power over the woman (here combining with Dracula's aristocratic dominance)[9] is continually reiterated

in the text, which gives far more space to the vampiric transform-
ations of the woman than those of the man. Male strength is thus
set against the usurping female power, and yet the important
distinction has to be made between Dracula's power over his
vampire women, which, for all its occasional violence, is largely
mesmeric, and the power of the male alliance between Harker and
his friends, which is the power of phallic violence and religious
fervour. This may be clearly realised in the scene where Arthur
drives the stake through Lucy's heart, to restore her as 'a holy, and
not an unholy memory' (p. 258):

> But Arthur never faltered. He looked like a figure of Thor as his
> untrembling arm rose and fell, driving deeper and deeper the
> mercy-bearing stake, while the blood from the pierced heart
> welled and spurted up around it. His face was set, and high duty
> seemed to shine through it . . . .   (p. 258)

Thor, the male deity (who married the woman as peasant),
opposes his phallic power against the 'voluptuous wantonness'
(pp. 252–3) of Lucy as vampire. Her newly found sexuality, to
which the text gives considerable emphasis, is set against the
holiness of the male mission accomplished by Van Helsing,
Seward and Arthur, a mission of 'infinite kindness' (p. 258) which
is achieved through a startling violation of the woman's body:

> Arthur placed the point over the heart, and as I looked I could
> see its dint in the white flesh. Then he struck with all his might.
>   The thing in the coffin writhed; and a hideous, blood-curdling
> screech came from the opened red lips. The body shook and
> quivered and twisted in wild contortions; the sharp white teeth
> champed together till the lips were out and the mouth was
> smeared with crimson foam.   (pp. 258–9)

The fear of Lucy, of the woman's 'whole carnal and unspiritual
appearance' (p. 256) (which *Dracula* equates with its anxieties about
the 'New Woman'[10]) is overcome in this scene by an odd mixture of
bourgeois scientific apparatus – Van Helsing's leather bag, oil
lamp, operating knives, coal hammer – and eroticised rape. It is
followed by the beheading, the symbolic castration divesting Lucy
of all sexual power.[11] Lucy has also been in rebellion against her
role as mother, dashing the child at her breast to the ground,

having nurtured herself with its blood, a pointed reversal of the expectations attached to her. It is this which leads to her attempted seduction of her lover, and the text thereby combines the feminine libido with 'unfeminine' practice in what evolves as a continuous equation of the 'natural' with the norms so forcefully articulated in the language of Harker and his friends.

This language circumscribes the knowledge held by the book's major narrators, and as a result they all consistently describe the woman vampire's metamorphosis (from passivity to sexual awareness) in terms which indicate female desire but articulate an aggression which is essentially phallocentric. The narrators' projections of sadistic sexual theories onto the woman no doubt derive from the contemporary obscurity of the woman's sexual life. As a consequence the female vampires are rendered by them as sexual aggressors sapping strength, a confused formulation further ratified by the satisfaction which accompanies their accounts of the exorcising ceremony of the driven stake, reversing the power struggle in terms that they find more acceptable. Thus Van Helsing fears the 'voluptuous beauty' which threatens his masculine strength in his fantasy: 'Then the beautiful eyes of the fair woman open and look love, and the voluptuous mouth present to a kiss – and man is weak' (p. 439). His identification of the weakening of the man with the sexual act, with all its attendant castration anxiety, can only be overcome by a reversal of the procedure in his butchering of the woman's body (see p. 441).

As can be seen, *Dracula* is a particularly sinister text in its pornographic tendency to aestheticise and eroticise sadistic rape, and it grasps at the sanctifying approval of a specifically Christian mission in doing so. Van Helsing 'wins the women's souls' for God in his butchering, and warms to his earlier tasks on Lucy's body in a peculiar litany with Arthur on their shared duty (pp. 247–8). When this is accomplished he moves into a particularly disturbing religious ecstasy (recalled also in Quincey Morris's dying words at the end of the novel) – a common feature of the psychopathic rapist's behaviour:

And now, my child, you may kiss her. Kiss her dead lips if you will, as she would have you to, if for her to choose. For she is not a grinning devil now – not any more a foul Thing for all eternity. No longer she is the devil's Un-Dead. She is God's true dead, whose soul is with Him! (p. 260).

It is significant that no such psychological complications are to be found in the case of the male vampire, Renfield, and, while Mina is clearly threatened with similar treatment to that received by Lucy, her salvation may well be associated with her masculine qualities (her androgyny is established by way of her 'man's brain' and her absorption of the steadfast 'moral' determination of her male friends).[12] Renfield, since he cannot represent a sexual challenge to the central values of the text, receives a unique kind of therapy, which is both scientific (confinement in the asylum) and religious. He responds to the latter in his dying confession to Van Helsing, wherein his essentially rational morality is clearly rendered: he has wrestled with Dracula, the agent of possession, and, further, he wishes to use his acquired knowledge for the altruistic purpose of retrieving Mina from the degradation suffered by Lucy.

Renfield is therefore a deviant rather than a mystified embodiment of the new power that Lucy represents. The battle for his soul does not necessitate the violation of his body, for his possession has been effected in desexualised terms. Dracula's assaults on him are blasphemous and not homosexual, and his relation of these encounters describes them in the forms of inverted religious rituals, beginning with the entry of the spirit, and culminating the eucharistic taking of blood for eternal life:

> I wouldn't ask him to come in at first though I knew he wanted to – just as he had wanted to all along. Then he began promising me things. . . . Then he began to whisper: 'Rats, rats, rats! Hundreds, thousands, millions of them, and every one a life; and dogs to eat them, and cats too. All lives! all red blood, with years of life in it; and not merely buzzing flies . . . All these lives I will give you, ay, and many more and greater, through countless ages, if you will fall down and worship me!' (pp. 332–3)

The text is decisive in reserving the terrible sexual revenge decreed by Van Helsing for its woman vampires. Dracula himself expires as if in combat (he is simply stabbed) and this unritualised ending is consistent with his representation as a Romantic hero; virile, unhappy, self-aware, and controlled. The noble Satanic hero is a stable masculine element whose plot finds familiar and established fictional procedures. In disposing of Dracula the novel has no need to wander into the ambivalence and symbolism which it creates in its dealings with the unfamiliar and mysterious rebellion of the feminine libido.

Dracula's role could be regarded simply as being the catalyst which awakens the woman's desire. His assaults do not take the same consistently violent forms as Van Helsing's remedies, and it is Van Helsing himself who proclaims plainly to Harker that 'your Vampire, though in all afterwards he can come when and how he will, must at the first make entry only when asked thereto by an inmate' (p. 360). This is a means whereby the text implies that the dangerous vampiric tendency lurks within all women, for Mina Harker, who succumbs to the seduction, is one of the Victorian novel's most classic embodiments of archetypal purity, the ideal bourgeois marriage-mate. And yet it is more than this also. It causes us to see Dracula as her lover, and to regard his role therefore, as developing beyond that of a simple catalyst.

Dracula's mesmeric powers may be the novel's means of displacing the recognition of a meeting between the desire of the woman and the desire of the man, for by this mystification it obstructs the investigation which requires to find the source of Mina's willingness. Yet precisely because it has created this problem for itself (Dracula's assaults could have been purely violent and unwelcomed) we can see that the novel makes space for the indication and recognition of the woman's desire without being able to reconcile itself to it. And thus it is, as I have argued above, that such desire will only be tentatively recognised, and will be described by a projection or extension of the sadistic terms which are centralised in the text's symbolic representations of the sexual act. Within this weakened and uncertain structure, which is almost submerged by *Dracula*'s main current, we can maintain a view of Mina as Dracula's lover. In their films, Murnau, and after him Herzog, retrieved this element of the text, and asserted the woman's sexuality, but only to the limited extent of allowing it to become the self-sacrifice ensuring Dracula's salvation through final death. In Stoker's text, the writing struggles to repress the possibilities for Mina that it unwillingly recognises, yet it does not quite succeed, for the only fully reported episode involving Dracula and Mina is richly ambiguous in its attempts to describe what is seen.

This is the moment when Dr Seward recounts the surprising of Dracula and Mina in her bedroom. He gives two conflicting accounts of what he sees: the first being that which he writes in his journal as his immediate impression as the group of men break open the door; the second when he relives the episode (again within the journal) in order to explain the events to Harker. Here is his first version:

> Kneeling on the near edge of the bed facing outwards was the white-clad figure of his wife. By her side stood a tall thin man, clad in black. His face was turned from us, but the instant we saw it we all recognized the Count – in every way, even to the scar on his forehead. With his left hand he held both Mrs Harker's hands, keeping them away with her arms at full tension; his right hand gripped her by the back of the neck, forcing her face down upon his bosom. Her white nightdress was smeared with blood, and a thin stream trickled down the man's bare breast, which was shown by his torn open dress.
>
> (p. 336)

Even here there are problems indicating the confused notion of what has been seen. What is described clearly occurs within an instant, and the succeeding events demonstrate that this tableau is only momentarily apprehended. Yet Seward will and will not see the Count's face: it is turned away, but he recognises the scar on his forehead. The slight confusion suggests the impulse of projection. Seward is unsure of what he has actually seen, as his vision is in fact created in the writing of his journal. The very act of writing (which ultimately belongs to Stoker) is Seward's means of evolving a fantasy, and this is more readily seen in his second account:

> I told how the ruthless hands of the Count had held his wife in that terrible and horrid position with her mouth to the open wound in his breast. It interested me, even at that moment, to see that whilst the face of white set passion worked convulsively over the bowed head, the hands tenderly and lovingly stroked the ruffled hair.   (p. 339)

Now Seward not only sees the face. He notes its expression of passion, and adds the feature of the hands stroking the hair. The perceptive reader will know that this is an impossibility according to the details of the first account. For, even if we accept that the hands might be Dracula's or Mina's, the first account showed Dracula's right hand holding her neck, and his left restraining both her hands away from his body. And 'that terrible position' is recalled again here, in the second account. The scene as now recognised represents a meeting of sadistic and affectionate theories of the sexual act: to Seward this is bewildering (his narratives are not infrequently punctuated by symptoms of his puzzlement) and he merely notes the fact without analysis. It is clear that he does not know what he has seen, or how to interpret it. Equally it may be that his conflicting accounts denote a dualistic interpretation, a segregation of conflicting elements which his limited awareness is unable to reconcile. The dilemma is a classic representation of the confusion which attends the Freudian child's discovery of his parents in the sexual act. This particular primal scene, with all its suggestions of fellatio, and the child's blundering entry into his parents' room, conflates the blood of the woman with the man's seminal fluid, and interprets their meeting in sadistic terms. [13] At the same time there is a strong sense of an act of deep affection (the stroking of the hair is a clear and immediately familiar gesture to the child) which cannot be equated with the sadistic fantasy, and needs, therefore, to be separated from what is seen, to the extent that it has to become a physical impossibility.

Whatever Murnau, and after him Herzog, made of this affection in the finale of each of their films, both directors did not shy away from the sexual paradox which, through Seward, the text lets slip. Although the possibility of other interpretations increases the complexity of the endings, I take it that these films frankly acknowledge Mina's masochistic eroticism, and thereby leave her firmly entrenched in the symbolic pattern structured around the woman as willing sacrificial victim. This pattern only grants the woman sexual power in so far as it offers salvation to the man, and the politics of this are unacceptable to most of us. Equally unacceptable, and probably more so, are the politics of Bram Stoker's text, which restores Lucy as the angelic and pure woman through the violence of sexual revenge, and manipulates Mina into the position of the secular domestic angel by dissipating her erotic experience, or relegating it into the perverse and evil. Thus she is saved by the messianic pure male, Quincey Morris, who dies 'a gallant gentleman' (p. 448) in the text's final placing of Mina as the bearer of children, a creature of 'sweetness and loving care' (p. 449).

Seward's paradoxical knowledge of Mina and Dracula points us to an important consistency within the novel. If the women vampires represent a dimly recognised but barely concealed sexual rebellion, rendered only through the partial knowledge of the 'normal' world, embodied in the narrators' common language, then Dracula too belongs to this rebellion. His assaults on the women, requiring their willingness, are therefore related to us with the vague perception that he has in fact crossed the boundary represented by the mirror. For all the mystification which the narrators' create around him, Dracula's invasion into their world succeeds in the case of Lucy, and almost in that of Mina too. By introducing the element of affection into Dracula's meeting with Mina, Seward may be acknowledging the passing of Dracula through the mirror into the world he accepts. The massive irony, of course, is that the violent world which he and the other narrators conceive for Dracula is actually a projection of their own hidden values so clearly depicted in the 'killing' of Lucy. Dracula does not have a mirror in which he could show the narrators the versions of self that are present in this ritual, but, if he did, then we can only suppose that they would also see nothing which they would be prepared to recognise.

Believing so securely in themselves, the narrators – with the exception of Mina – see the other in essentially limited terms. Just as they expect to see the commonly conceived and predictable self in the mirror, so too they see the otherness of women in terms only of the self. Yet Seward's reflection of what he sees on breaking into Mina's bedroom does imply the presence of a knowledge in the struggles of its birth, for he detects not only the certainty of affection within an otherwise anxiously conceived theory of sexuality, but also something more far-reaching in Dracula's self-mutilation. It is true that Dracula's act of forcing Mina to drink from his wound may be another equation of the sexual act with castration (seen already in Harker's encounter with the three vampires and Van Helsing's words quoted above). But equally this may be a peculiar registration of Dracula representing the otherness of androgyny, the sexuality that denies phallocentric power in its mutilation, taking on thereby the role of the woman as conceived by the narrators. For this is a sexuality which looks like domination, but is not seen to be quite so simple in Seward's second glance, which reveals both mutual exchange (the drinkings of each other's blood) and affection.

The Victorian novel that has been established and typified through the moulding of a great tradition is commonly regarded as a text organised according to the weight of its author's moral deliberation, delivered either through direct authorial commentary, or through the mouthpiece of a central character. That *Dracula* does not do this may be one reason for its neglect, to which could be added that it shows no interest in the development of character and psychology (as do the works of Dickens, James and Eliot). For this novel belongs to a submerged and alternative tradition, that of Gothic and post-Gothic mystery, wherein the moral centre is given and unquestioned (here the goodness of Harker and his associates) and opposed to the unpredictable mystery of insoluble crime of unmotivated evil. Such texts permit the access of unstable elements into the chemistry of the novel, blending conventional fictive procedures with less predictable and potentially chaotic agencies. The threat to the moral centre of the novel is beyond complete intelligibility; it is deliberately mystified, and remains so, despite the attempted exorcism by a dependence on a conventional *dénouement*. In the case of *Dracula* the novel's conventional veneer (the triumph of goodness) is achieved so awkwardly that we are bound to probe this morality established through ritualised violence, discovering in the process that there is a highly suggestive reciprocity between the projection of mystified evil (Dracula's violent sexuality) and the means of exorcising it (the ceremony of the driven stake). The equivalence discloses something of the derivation of *Dracula*'s motifs, which I have taken as unconsciously organised symbols denoting a fear of female sexuality and at the same time a tentatively realised acknowledgement of the massive complexity of the libido. To attribute this to Stoker himself is too simple, as is the suggestion that *Dracula* is yet another key to the clichéd notion of repressed Victorian sexuality. The text is not a transparent medium granting access to the author or his society: it is a highly wrought complex of conventions taken from differing sources which reacts with the ideologies of author and period. This process itself is far too involved and mysterious to be precisely decoded. What my analysis is attempting is to decipher the symbolic structures which are thrown up in the reaction. In requiring us to place our trust as readers in the integrity of their language, the book's narrators are requiring too much, for what they denote is so much more than they ever write.

Notes

1. David Punter, *The Literature of Terror: A History of Gothic Fictions from 1765 to the Present Day* (London: Longman, 1980) p. 256.
2. Walter Benjamin, *Illuminations* (London: Fontana, 1973) pp. 231–2.
3. Ibid., p. 231.
4. Ibid.
5. Ibid., p. 232.
6. Page references relate to Bram Stoker, *Dracula* (Harmondsworth: Penguin, 1979) p. 449. All quotations from the novel are from this edition.
7. See Jacques Lacan, 'The Mirror Stage as Formative of the Function of the I as Revealed in Psychoanalytic Experience', in *Écrits: A Selection*, tr. Alan Sheridan (London: Tavistock, 1977).
8. Sigmund Freud, *On Sexuality* (1905) in *The Pelican Freud Library*, ed. J. Strachey, vii (Harmondsworth: Penguin, 1977) 269.
9. For an expansion of this theme see Punter, *The Literature of Terror*, pp. 256–62.
10. See Geoffrey Wall, ' "Different from Writing": *Dracula* in 1897', *Literature and History*, 10, no. 1 (Spring 1984) 16.
11. Freud, *On Sexuality*, p. 281.
12. Wall, in *Literature and History*, 10, no. 1, p. 16.
13. For Freud's explication of this theory, see Freud, *On Sexuality*, pp. 198–200, and the case history of the 'Wolf Man' in *Case Histories II*, *The Pelican Freud Library*, ix (Harmondsworth: Penguin, 1979).

7

Arthur Conan Doyle's *The Parasite*: the Case of the Anguished Author

ANNE CRANNY-FRANCIS

In 1894, the year of publication of *The Parasite*, Arthur Conan Doyle was a successful and wealthy writer, who moved among the middlebrow mainstream of contemporary English culture. For literary companionship he looked to Jerome K. Jerome, Robert Barr and James M. Barrie, rather than Oscar Wilde and Aubrey Beardsley. As Charles Higham notes in his biography of Conan Doyle, the author's 'large figure and military manner' would have seemed 'hopelessly provincial and alienating' to those who frequented the circles emanating from the aesthetic magazine, *The Yellow Book*, 'the silken young men, most of whom were far too effeminate and weedy for his robust taste'.[1]

Conan Doyle's reputation was based on the Sherlock Holmes adventures, those pseudo-scientific triumphs of rationalism over the forces of evil endemic to large urban centres such as London. In fact, the popularity of Holmes was so great and the pressure on Conan Doyle to keep producing new adventures for his hero so consistent and heavy that, in late 1893, Doyle killed him off. In a struggle to the finish Holmes and Moriarty plunge over the huge and magnificent Reichenbach Falls – a strangely Romantic end, one might think, for a hero of rationalism.

Of course, one of the most interesting aspects of Holmes was his ambiguity, the contradictions built into his characterisation which constantly threaten to undermine his rationalism. Holmes is a drug addict; in 'The Sign of Four' he injects himself with cocaine in front of an amazed and horrified Doctor Watson. Holmes stores his pipe tobacco in such eccentric places as the toe of a Persian slipper, and his cigars in a coal-scuttle. He is notoriously untidy and Doctor Watson notes in 'The Musgrave Ritual' that unanswered mail was 'transfixed by a jack-knife into the very centre of his wooden mantle-piece'.[2] Add to this Holmes's exotic smoking-jackets, his fondness for playing the violin at odd times (badly), his love of disguise, and his rejection or repression of the 'softer passions'[3] and the picture is less that of a rationalist than of one of the most celebrated eccentrics produced in English literature.

Yet the rationalist discourse consistently dominates the description and perception of Holmes – as it did the lives of middle-class readers and writers in late-nineteenth-century Britain. At the same time, however, those lives were constantly assailed by doubt. Traditional and more recent beliefs were under challenge. Darwinism had shaken or even destroyed the assumption that humanity was in some way the end point or final grand product of creation. Indeed, for many, it destroyed belief in creation itself – and so belief in God, divinity and Christianity. Britain's loss of technological dominance in the late nineteenth century was an equally bitter blow. For those who assimilated Darwinism as Social Darwinism, it was especially so – signifying the degeneration of the British nation. Simultaneously Britain lost its hold on the imperialist dominance of underdeveloped nations. In the course of the nineteenth century Germany and the United States had also advanced technologically until they had overtaken Britain, which by the end of the century was plagued by outdated equipment and processes. Now Germany and the United States were able to challenge Britain for control of the less technologically advanced nations, which often provided the raw materials for production processes. This imperialist competition often meant that claims had to be established on territory before its economic viability was carefully considered. This was an expensive operation and often resulted in poor returns. By the last decade of the nineteenth century Britain had been in recession for almost twenty years; this was the period historians often call the 'Great Depression'. Its consequences were not only economic but also, perhaps more importantly, social.[4]

By the last decade of the nineteenth century the combination of a number of factors – urbanisation of the population, the economic practices of capitalism, and the depression of the 1830s and 40s and later of the 1870s and 1890s – had impressed on workers both the possibility and the expediency of their acting in solidarity. To the middle classes this represented a serious threat to their social and political domination. The writing of socialists such as Karl Marx, who attributed middle-class dominance of society to such environmental factors as their access to capital and their consequent control of such social institutions as the press, judiciary, schools and government, also challenged notions of the biological superiority of the middle classes – an idea based in Social Darwinism, which compensated handsomely for the loss of creationist supremacy.

The political threat from working-class union or 'Labour' was often allied to another, the social and political challenge posed by the 'New Woman', the emancipist. The demands of women for social and political recognition and representation were seen as a threat to the institutions of Victorian society. The popularity of Annie Besant's pamphlet on contraception, for example, was regarded as one result of the increasing sexual awareness of women – one which might result in the extinction of the family, perhaps society itself. The aesthetes were often regarded as the male counterparts of the emancipists, their effete mannerisms and sexual ambiguity perhaps as great a threat to the future of the family and society.[5]

All these groups – workers, women, aesthetes – were involved in an interrogative process, challenging the veracity or infallibility of aspects of the patriarchal, bourgeois-dominated society of the late nineteenth century. This challenge might be directed at the power of the middle classes or at the sexual stereotyping of men and women in that society. In either case the challenge ultimately rested with the institutions and practices which perpetuated those behavioural patterns, value systems and beliefs.

This environment, a society struggling for domestic security and international dominance but torn by doubts and internal contradictions, was a fertile breeding-ground for the new science of psychology, the study of the mind and of behaviour. The science of psychology is represented by Conan Doyle as a catalytic element in his strange story *The Parasite*, published in 1894 shortly after the demise of the redoubtable Holmes. In this novel Conan Doyle expresses the contradictions within his society with the same power as, though less self-consciousness than, the decadent artists of *The Yellow Book*. Their productions were often intended to outrage the bourgeoisie, to shock them out of their complacency about their economic/social/political/sexual roles and behaviour. Conan Doyle's story, on the other hand, dramatises the tenuousness of that complacency, its volatility, and the practices by which it is maintained.

The Parasite tells the story of Professor Gilroy, a young and ambitious scientist whose speciality is physiology. At thirty-four he is one of the youngest people ever to be given a university chair, and he is very aware of the resulting professional and social pressures. As befitting an eminent scientist, Gilroy is extremely sceptical about areas of study or knowledge not recognised as scientific or 'objective'. At the same time, however, he does acknowledge the conservatism of the scientific community towards disciplines not yet fully established and institutionalised: for example, the psychological research of his friend Wilson. One evening Wilson invites Gilroy to his home to meet a woman said to be a skilled mesmerist or hypnotist. Gilroy is extremely distrustful of the medium, Miss Penelosa, a woman of West Indian extraction. Gilroy is subsequently convinced of Miss Penelosa's credibility when she plants a post-hypnotic suggestion in the mind of Gilroy's fiancée, Agatha, that she should terminate their engagement the following morning. When Gilroy later questions Agatha about the incident, he finds that she has no recollection of having left her home that day. As a result he decides to carry out a series of experiments in which he is hypnotised by Miss Penelosa – in order to determine the physiological and mental properties of the mesmeric state. Gradually Gilroy realises that Miss Penelosa is taking control of his actions. Worse, she is forcing him to act towards her as a lover. When Gilroy rejects Miss Penelosa's advances, she expresses her revenge by causing him to give absurd lectures (which results in his suspension), to rob a bank and to assault a colleague who had also rejected her advances. The final provocation comes when Gilroy finds himself in his fiancée's bedroom holding a bottle of sulphuric acid. He surmises that Penelosa had intended him to throw it in Agatha's face, as an act of jealous spite. Distraught, demoralised, and physically enfeebled, Gilroy decides he must kill his tormentor. He arrives at her lodgings to find that she died at the moment he woke from his trance in Agatha's room.

The Parasite is not an easy novel to obtain and is not often critically discussed. In an article entitled 'The Case of the Great Detective',[6] Stephen Knight suggests that the reasons for its obscurity lie with the author himself. Knight claims that, under pressure from Conan Doyle, the book had only two early reprints and one US edition – this at a time when Conan Doyle's works were enormously popular. Knight also claims that Conan Doyle dropped the book from the list of publications which appeared at the front of his books. While some critics have related Conan Doyle's actions to the critique of spiritualism in the book, Knight suggests rather that it is the book's overt discussion of sexuality and sexual obsession which concerned the author. Charles Higham agrees:

> Later disowned by him, and virtually ignored by his biographers, the work remains a strikingly personal revelation of neurotic sexual obsession, reminiscent of Poe but nevertheless expressive of Conan Doyle's mysterious and highly individual character as an artist.[7]

Certainly there were some personal reasons for interest in this subject in 1894. The previous year his first wife, Louise, had been diagnosed as having turberculosis, and sexual abstinence was part of her treatment. Since Conan Doyle lived by a code of conduct which forbade outside affairs (it is noteworthy that he really did, it seems, live by this code, rather than simply subscribe to it publicly and flout it privately, as did so many Victorians),[8] it may be that he was sexually frustrated when he wrote The Parasite. It seems that his grief over Louise's illness may have been compounded with guilt – that, as a qualified doctor, he had not recognised her symptoms earlier and had insisted she accompany him on a number of holidays and excursions which probably exacerbated the effect of the disease. The combination of sexual frustration and guilt seems a likely catalyst for the production of such a tale. Yet The Parasite is much more than a documented personal confession: it is an intriguing and powerful piece of fiction and deserves discussion as such.

The theme of sexuality is evident in The Parasite from the opening paragraphs:

> March 24th. – The spring is fairly with us now. Outside my laboratory window the great chestnut-tree is all covered with the big glutinous gummy buds, some of which have already begun to break into little green shuttle-cocks. . . . The wet earth smells fruitful and luscious. Green shoots are peeping out everywhere. The twigs are stiff with their sap. . . . Buds in the hedges, lambs beneath them – everywhere the work of reproduction going forward!

I can see it without and I can feel it within. We also have our spring when the little arterioles dilate, the lymph flows in a brisker stream, the glands work harder, winnowing and straining.   (pp. 1–2)[9]

This joyous evocation of the fruitful spring, with its scarcely veiled sexual references, is echoed in the description of Gilroy's fiancée, 'who was looking charming in white and pink with glittering wheat-ears in her hair' (pp. 8–9). The connection between youth, beauty, the natural world, spring and innocent sexuality is maintained. The description of Miss Penelosa stands in marked contrast:

Any one less like my idea of a West Indian could not be imagined. She was a small, frail creature, well over forty, I should say, with a pale, peaky face, and hair of a very light shade of chestnut. Her presence was insignificant and her manner retiring. . . . Her eyes were perhaps her most remarkable, and also, I am compelled to say, her least pleasant feature. They were grey in colour – grey with a shade of green – and their expression struck me as being decidedly furtive. . . . On second thoughts, feline would have expressed it better. A crutch leaning against the wall told me, what was painfully evident when she rose, that one of her legs was crippled.   (pp. 11–12).

The details of Miss Penelosa's physical description are highly significant. As a West Indian Miss Penelosa was assumed by Gilroy to be dark, her 'otherness' or alienness in the British context making her exotic. But Miss Penelosa is pale and insignificant – not sufficiently 'different' to be exotic – and yet still an alien. Her eyes, traditionally 'the mirror of the soul', are a bilious colour and have a deceitful, cunning expression. This feature adds a suggestion of evil to her character which is emphasised, in this context, by her age and deformity. With his opening description of spring and his later portrait of Agatha, Conan Doyle produces an environment of health, vigour and beauty – into which Miss Penelosa comes as a kind of blight, a kind of alien evil. As the narrative develops, the nature of that evil starts to become clear. Significantly the revelation begins in an incident involving Agatha. When Agatha gives Miss Penelosa permission to hypnotise her, Gilroy observes that

Miss Penelosa undergoes a transformation. In the act of exercising her power her eyes glow, her cheeks gain colour and she seems to increase in stature. And Gilroy notes also his resentment at the attitude with which she regards the prone Agatha: 'the expression with which a Roman empress might have looked at her kneeling slave' (p. 16). Miss Penelosa is revealed as a creature who feeds on power. Her attitude to Agatha and the nature of her post-hypnotic suggestion alert the reader that this power may be sexual in essence.

Agatha, on the other hand, is never explicitly associated with sexuality. Conan Doyle includes several incidents in the narrative which are meant to confirm Agatha as a conventionally naïve, sexually unaware middle-class Victorian woman. For example, when Gilroy visits Agatha to reassure himself about their engagement on the morning after the meeting with Miss Penelosa, Agatha insists that she has been at home all morning – though at one stage, she confesses, she fell asleep, while reading a French novel. Reading steamy novels by French writers was regarded as a characteristic of the 'New Woman'; from them, it was believed, she acquired her sexual precocity. That Agatha was bored by a French novel indicates her conventional innocence and naïveté. Later, when Gilroy is firmly in Miss Penelosa's power, he remembers that they have discussed Agatha: 'Miss Penelosa said that she was conventional, and I agreed with her' (p. 54). A fundamental characteristic of female conventionality at the time was sexual naïveté. So it does not seem plausible to understand Miss Penelosa as in any way associated with Agatha – as a repressed, evil side in the Jekyll and Hyde mould. Rather Miss Penelosa is associated with the men in the narrative, principally Gilroy.

In order to establish the role Miss Penelosa plays in the narrative, it is useful to trace the development of Gilroy's response to her. He first becomes aware of Miss Penelosa as a pernicious influence when he realises that she is manipulating him into making love to her. Though fascinated by her power, Gilroy is physically repelled by her:

She is far older than myself, and a cripple. It is monstrous – odious, – and yet the impulse was so strong that had I stayed another minute in her presence I should have committed myself.
(pp. 49–50)

Nevertheless, Gilroy realises that he is becoming more and more deeply involved with her – allowing her to criticise Agatha and finding himself constantly on the brink of transferring his allegiances from Agatha to her:

> It is monstrous, but it is true. Again, to-night, I awoke from the mesmeric trance to find my hand in hers, and to suffer that odious feeling which urges me to throw away my honour, my career – everything – for the sake of this creature who, as I can plainly see when I am away from her influence, possesses no single charm upon earth.   (pp. 53–4)

Miss Penelosa, it seems, has become an obsession with him. One evening Gilroy decides to break his usual appointment with her – to no avail. Halfway through the evening he is gripped by an overpowering urge to visit her, a compulsion so strong that he no longer feels in contact with reality. He is aware of his surroundings as he hurries to the Wilsons' only 'as in a dream': 'It was all misty and strange and unnatural' (p. 57). After this visit Gilroy is left with one strong impression:

> I hardly recall what we talked about, but I do remember that Miss Penelosa shook the head of her crutch at me in a playful way, and accused me of being late and of losing interest in our experiments.   (p. 57)

The crutch operates from then on as an overt phallic symbol, and it becomes the focus of Gilroy's obsession:

> And could her influence not reach me in Persia and bring me back to within touch of her crutch?   (p. 63)

> I had never particularly observed before what sort of sound the tapping of a crutch was.... (p. 87)

> She tapped with her crutch on the floor.   (p. 90)

> An instant later she was gone, and I heard the quick hobble and tap receding down the passage.   (p. 91)

In a phallocentric, patriarchal society the phallus signifies absolute power. That Gilroy is totally controlled by this phallus-wielding figure indicates that he has somehow lost control over his own sexuality, that he is obsessed with sexuality as a force, as power, and that this threatens to disrupt his understanding/perception of reality itself. And the picture is even more complex – since the figure with the phallus is not only female but also *within* Gilroy.

The interiority of this evil figure is confirmed in the title of the novel, which Gilroy subsequently confers on Miss Penelosa: 'She can project herself into my body and take command of it. She has a parasitic soul – yes, she is a parasite, a monstrous parasite' (p. 60). Prior to this Gilroy has begun to feel her influence as possession: 'I could almost believe the tales of obsession by evil spirits, so overmastering was the impulse' (p. 50). At first Gilroy suspects that this evil is part of his own nature, something usually kept hidden: 'She rouses something in me – something evil – something I had rather not think of' (p. 54). As the narrative progresses, however, Gilroy gradually isolates those evil impulses, transferring them to Miss Penelosa:

> There is some consolation in the thought, then, that these odious impulses for which I have blamed myself do not really come from me at all. They are all transferred from her, little as I could have guessed it at the time. I feel cleaner and lighter for the thought.   (p. 59)

Now when they become active in him, he perceives himself as possessing a 'peculiar double consciousness':

> There was the predominant alien will, which was bent upon drawing me to the side of its owner, and there was the feebler protesting personality, which I recognised as being myself, tugging feebly at the overmastering impulse as a led terrier might at its chain, I can remember recognising these two conflicting forces, but I recall nothing of my walk....
> (pp. 75–6)

In describing this process by which Gilroy attempts to come to terms with, or rationalise, his problem Conan Doyle reproduces as well as reveals the mechanisms of sexual repression in late Victorian society.

In *Totem and Taboo*[10] Freud writes about the mechanisms of repression and obsession, noting that, when an act is prohibited, it is not abolished but rather driven into the unconscious. There it persists as an unfulfilled desire in constant tension with the prohibition: the result is a 'psychical fixation'. A characteristic of this psychological configuration or 'constellation' is what Freud describes as the subject's 'ambivalent attitude' towards the act involved in the repression. For example, if a child is instructed to avoid certain acts of touching, 'he is constantly wishing to perform this act (the touching), [and looks on it as his supreme enjoyment, but he must not perform it] and detests it as well'.[11] In *The Parasite* Gilroy, a rational Victorian male, a scientist, feels the power of sexual need. In his society, however, sexual activity before marriage is denied him. His sexual desire is repressed, driven unfulfilled into his unconscious where it exists in an uneasy tension with the prohibitions which prevent its expression. But the repressive apparatus begins to break down and Gilroy is involved in a kind of sexual experimentation. The desire, like Dr Jekyll's evil side, begins to manifest itself – as Miss Penelosa, or rather as Gilroy's desire for a sexual partner. Yet, as Freud explains, the result of repression is that the desired act is hated at the same time as it is the source of great enjoyment.

> I am, for the moment, at the beck and call of this creature with the crutch. I must come when she wills it. I must do as she wills. Worst of all, I must feel as she wills. I loathe her and fear her, yet while I am under the spell she can doubtless make me love her.
>
> (p. 59)

Gilroy's hatred of Miss Penelosa, of his own sexual desire, is a function of the sexual repression endemic to his society. Unable to accept the notion that such evil or transgression can be a part of his real self, Gilroy isolates it – as the other half of a 'double consciousness'. Gilroy creates/describes himself as a dual or split personality. But this, too, is unsatisfactory, given his need to see himself as a rational, objective, stable and consistent being (like Holmes?). Gilroy finally solves his problem by projecting this evil outside himself, onto the woman involved in the act. He then feels 'cleaner and lighter', while she becomes the source of all evil, of *his* evil. If she is then destroyed, or somehow eliminated, then his evil and his guilt will disappear – until the next time. This repressive process was common in Conan Doyle's society. Poverty-stricken working-class women forced into prostitution were commonly represented as the source of sexual evil in that society – rather than the patriarchal structure which circumscribed and delimited the lives and sexual needs of men and women. Conan Doyle does not explicitly criticise this practice in *The Parasite*, but he does reproduce it with unusual clarity. Further, he explores the consequences of living in such a consistently repressive situation.

Before I continue with this discussion it is important to note that no clear resolution occurs in Conan Doyle's text. Miss Penelosa dies before Gilroy can destroy her. Perhaps it is significant that he wakes from his trance during the visit of a clergyman. I think it is more likely, however, that Conan Doyle could find no solution to this problem. The obsession departs as mysteriously as it arrived – and no answers to the questions of its control and eradication are given. This final lack of resolution is one of the strengths and unconventionalities of *The Parasite*.

In exploring the consequences of prolonged repression, Doyle confronts the possibility that the individual may lose all awareness of her or his obsessive state and of the forces motivating her or his actions. Miss Penelosa herself reveals this level of command early in the book: 'it is possible for an operator to gain complete command over his subject' (p. 35). Later Gilroy rues his failure to heed Penelosa's own warning: 'Did she not herself warn me? Did she not tell me, as I can read in my own journal, that when she has acquired power over a subject she can make him do her will?' (pp. 58–9). Further he recalls her claim that when her power is strongly exerted the subject 'is absolutely unconscious' (p. 61). Towards the end of the narrative Gilroy finds himself in just such a state, either consciously or unconsciously compelled to act according to the dictates of an outside force. Interestingly, this process describes not only sexual obsession and repression, but repressive forces generally.

At the beginning of this essay I noted that, at the time *The Parasite* was written, Victorian society was in a highly volatile state – attempting to exert itself as an aggressive, unified world power, yet crossed and fissured by internal conflicts and dissensions. It was a time of great social contrasts – between rich and poor, men and women – and of equally strong ambiguity. More than anything else, it was a time of insecurity, of a felt need for the stability eaten away by recession and the successive intellectual, emotional and religious crises produced by new theories and beliefs and the debunking of old ones. In *The Parasite* Conan Doyle attempts to explore one of those areas of insecurity, the perception of sexuality and sex roles in his society. Significantly, honestly, he comes to no (re)solution. He states his fear at the power of sexuality – or, more correctly, of the repression of sexuality – to control and direct an individual's actions. This was the kind of awareness to which many of the new fields of study pointed. Psychology, for example, showed that people's actions, and even their thoughts, could be determined and directed by that very thing – their sexuality and its repression by social forces and institutions. The emancipist movement, meantime, was showing how people's perceptions of themselves and of others was determined by their sex and by conventional sex roles – which they related to economic, social and political factors. Socialists were showing how the behaviour of individuals was influenced by their class background. In other words, any notion of the autonomy of the individual was finally challenged and laid to rest in this period. The effect of this realisation on the individual could be quite devastating: it might even challenge one's perception of 'reality' itself.

In *The Parasite* Conan Doyle reproduces this fundamental confusion. *The Parasite* is not just about obsession; it is obsessive. In attempting to discover the process of sexual obsession, Conan Doyle recognises the use by the obsessive subject of the notion of dualism; she or he is split into a good, 'real' self and an evil, alien self. But this is not the only dualism described in the text. A non-exhaustive list would include psychology/science (p. 4), subjective/objective (p. 4), materialism/spirituality (pp. 4–5), male/female (p. 5), appearance/temperament (p. 5), fact and proof/surmise and fancy (p. 5), brute/dupe (p. 10), mind/imagination (p. 41), mind/matter (p. 47), intellect/psyche (p. 60), natural/supernatural (p. 70), love/hate (p. 79). The number of dualisms employed in the opening pages is particularly noteworthy. It seems that Conan Doyle's attempt to encompass one particular problem, that of sexuality, begins a process of continual displacement. In *Totem and Taboo* Freud writes of this displacement procedure:

> The ease with which the prohibition can be transferred and extended reflects a process which falls in with the unconscious desire and is greatly facilitated by the psychological conditions that prevail in the unconscious. The instinctual desire is constantly shifting in order to escape from the *impasse* and endeavours to find substitutes – substitute objects and substitute acts – in place of the prohibited ones.[12]

Conan Doyle's seemingly obsessive production of dualisms performs this same function. What is important here is not so much
the nature of the dualisms produced – they are mostly very
conventional – but their number and their importance in the
narrative. They are, in fact, what the narrative is about – about
continual displacement, about insecurity, loss of autonomy, help-
lessness in the face of unknown and imperceptible social forces.
Even science, the foremost discipline of the technological age, is
revealed as 'full of unreasoning prejudices' (p. 32). Conan Doyle's
exploration of sexual repression and its consequences reveals the
means by which the ideological practices of a society are maintained. The individual is not even aware of their operation – even
when they repress the most natural or fundamental needs and
desires. The inconclusive ending of *The Parasite* expresses the
difficulty faced by the individual who attempts to locate her or his
place within the social structure, with its many and conflicting
institutions and practices. The result is most likely to be the
continuous displacement formally reproduced in the narrative – a
perpetual series of reflections, mirrors within mirrors, with reality
located not in one particular reflection, but in the process of
reflection

In *The Parasite* Conan Doyle attempts to confront the uncertain-
ties which gave the rationalism of Holmes its attractiveness and
piquancy. Whereas in the Holmes stories Conan Doyle fore-
grounded the rationalist discourse, in *The Parasite* the rationalist
discourse is challenged – in the character of a brilliant and eminent
scientist, Professor Gilroy – and found lacking. Conan Doyle
foregrounds not one particular discourse, but the disillusion with
many. The obsessional displacement process evident in the text
describes the way in which individuals attempt to deal with this
disillusion – and their almost inevitable failure.

Writing *The Parasite* must have been cathartic for Conan Doyle.
Personally it was an expression of the sexual frustration which was
a problem in his own life. On another level, however, it exorcised
the ghost of Holmes, the eccentric rationalist. It expressed the
problems, crises, doubts which made Holmes a neurotic eccentric
and explained the process to which he subjected himself in order to
be, sometimes, a rationalist. Essentially *The Parasite* exposed the
falseness of the rationalist position – that its maintenance was
based on the rigid enforcement of economically and politically
determined norms, beliefs, values, behavioural practices not

necessarily susceptible to rational analysis. Rosemary Jackson, writing of the relationship between the fantastic and the real or rational, notes the interrogative character of fantasy:

> Anti-rational, it is the inverse side of reason's orthodoxy. It reveals reason and reality to be arbitrary, shifting constructs, and thereby scrutinizes the category of the 'real'. Contradictions surface and are held antinomically in the fantastic text, as reason is made to confront all that it traditionally refuses to encounter. The structure of fantastic narrative is one founded upon contradictions.[13]

By these criteria Arthur Conan Doyle's novel *The Parasite* must qualify as one of the most innovative fantasies of the late nineteenth century.

Notes

1. Charles Higham, *The Adventures of Conan Doyle: The Life of the Creator of Sherlock Holmes* (London: Hamish Hamilton, 1976) p. 104.
2. Quoted ibid., p. 109.
3. Arthur Conan Doyle, 'A Scandal in Bohemia', quoted in Ronald Pearsall, *Conan Doyle: A Biographical Solution* (London: Weidenfeld and Nicolson, 1977) p. 58.
4. On the economic, social and political environment of nineteenth-century Britain see E. J. Hobsbawm, *Industry and Empire: From 1750 to the Present Day*, in *The Pelican Economic History of Britain*, III (Harmondsworth: Pelican, 1969); Richard Shannon, *The Crisis of Imperialism 1865–1915* (St Albans: Paladin, 1974). On Social Darwinism see Raymond Williams, 'Social Darwinism', *Problems in Materialism and Culture: Selected Essays* (London: Verso, 1980).
5. Linda Dowling, 'The Decadent and the New Woman in the 1890s' *Nineteenth-Century Fiction*, 33 (1979) 434–53.
6. Stephen Knight, 'The Case of the Great Detective', *Meanjin*, 40, no. 2 (1981) 175–85.
7. Higham, *The Adventures of Conan Doyle*, p. 124.
8. Ibid., pp. 148–9; Pearsall, *Conan Doyle*, pp. 76–7.
9. Page references relate to Arthur Conan Doyle, *The Parasite* (London: Constable, 1894). All quotations from the novel are from this edition.
10. Sigmund Freud, 'Taboo and Emotional Ambivalence', in *Totem and Taboo* (London: Ark, 1983) pp. 18–74.
11. Ibid., p. 29.
12. Ibid., p. 30.
13. Rosemary Jackson, *Fantasy: The Literature of Subversion* (London: Methuen, 1981) p. 21.

8

The Lost World: Conan Doyle and the Suspense of Evolution

HOWARD DAVIES

> *Charles Darwin was such a fantasy spinner in his childhood that everyone thought him to be a worse fibber than Munchausen.*[1]

The Lost World, being an account of the recent amazing adventures of Professor E. Challenger, Lord John Roxton, Professor Summerlee and Mr Ed. Malone of the 'Daily Gazette'[2] is a text as worthy of exploration as was the territory itself. To reach the isolated plateau in Amazonas, on which fortuitous geological changes have ensured the survival of Jurassic flora and fauna, Professor Challenger's intrepid party deploys the intellectual apparatus of its time; it has at its disposal Darwinian evolutionary theory backed up by the sophisticated taxonomies of the natural sciences, as well as the 'vision of delirium' expressed in the water-colours of a previous traveller, the sole known Western witness of prehistoric life forms. My position is similar: the lost world is that of 1912, the date at which it became possible for Conan Doyle to imagine both this prehistory and a Professor Challenger capable of visiting it. My intellectual baggage, which I declare here at the frontier, as it were, consists of a conceptual debt to Freud, to Lévi-Strauss and to Sartre, together with recognition of the contribution to Conan Doyle studies made by Catherine Belsey.[3]

Time travel, after all, is not the prerogative of fictions and fantasies generated by exact scientists. What the French call the *sciences humaines* are just as capable, and perhaps more so, of transporting the reader into different perceptions of temporality. Malcolm Bowie quotes a remark of the exiled Freud that is extremely apposite in the present context: 'With neurotics it is as though we were in a prehistoric landscape – for instance, in the Jurassic. The great saurians are still running about; the horsetails grow as high as palms.'[4] Indeed, the pilgrimage made by Professor Challenger in 1912 to the origin of the species is repeated by Freud one year later in the wholly different theoretical context of *Totem and Taboo*. Subsequently, Lévi-Strauss too sets out for *le monde perdu* of the Nambikwara Indians (in chapter 24 of *Tristes Tropiques*), leaving the *carrefour* Réaumur–Sébastopol much as Professor Challenger had struck out from Enmore Park, West Kensington. Both psychoanalysis and structuralist anthropology ascribe great importance to the quest for origins: my intention here is to use them to help pose the questions of how Conan Doyle's *Lost World* constitutes its implied reader and what sort of community this implied reader could inhabit.

Fiction, falsehood, fantasy, ideology, science: it is by virtue of a segmentation of this continuum and of a ranking of the segments that *The Lost World* acquires its representational depth and perspective. Munchausen (*sic*) is invoked as negative exemplar in the second chapter, in which the cub reporter and narrator is urged by his editor to expose the eccentric scientist Challenger as a teller of tall tales. Accordingly, it is within a fiction conventionally claiming the status of fact that an apparent fiction is subjected to an adventurous process of empirical verification. The modern reader, if he or she is prepared to accept this convention and read on, does so, it seems to me, in order to see what gap there might be between the reader that the text appears to require and the reader as practitioner informed by recent developments in literary theory. This project is likewise an adventure inasmuch as it embarks upon a journey of over seventy years, a journey back into an English culture which is likely to be characterised by all the simultaneous strangeness and familiarity of that which has been long left behind.

Literary criticism since Barthes, persuaded of its own lack of specificity and motivated by an almost carnal sense of solidarity with that which it studies, operates within a logic of chiasmus, flirting with tautology and seduced by paradox. This is because the critic too is a teller of tales, but one who is informed of the capacity of narrative linearity to represent pasts and futures appropriate to the present and whose delectation derives from identifications that go beyond the characters represented and focus finally on the agent of representation, the author. In the context of this problematic *The Lost World* is a delight: parasitic on the narrative of evolutionism, it cannot but fascinate readers with an interest in species of mythic origins and in senses of endings.

In which literary community, then, is the reader required to conduct fieldwork in this instance? That of which Conan Doyle is founding father and to which he is doomed to cede his preeminence, namely the four males nominated in the sub-title: Professor E. Challenger, who, needless to say, professes and challenges; Professor Summerlee, from the groves of academe untimely ripp'd; Lord John Roxton, jack of all aristocratic pursuits from the Albany to Amazonas; and young Mr Ed. Malone, upon whom will appropriately devolve the narratorial and editorial function initiated authorially. The literary progenitor is separated from his offspring by the fact that, while they are 'within' the text, he is 'without' it, having surrendered it to them. Not only, however, is the apparent capacity for textual production transmitted from the first generation to the second, but a particular institutional agency is required to ratify this transmission of powers. This agency can only be the readership: it is detached, in so far as it has never previously been a party to transactions between the persons named above and has neither title nor direct claim to the estate transacted; but it is dependent, in so far as it is of the same species and is thus related genealogically to author and characters.

I should add that, if I, as participant observer in a Doylean primal horde, being of the nth generation and writing in my present, act as witness and mediator of the (d)evolutionary succession of author by narrator, I do so in obedience to epigraphic injunction. For, between title and first chapter, Conan Doyle bids farewell to his text and enters a state of latency and of apparent extinction in order that his text might evolve. Carefully, however, he preselects the readership appropriate to his purpose and does so in the following manner:

> I have wrought my simple plan
>   If I give one hour of joy
> To the boy who's half a man
>   Or the man who's half a boy.

This generous intent is a good articulation of the ideology of creation: he who creates gives, but in giving creates a potential recipient who must then be persuaded that receipt is advantageous. It is for the recipient to take it or leave it, it seems, (since no one compels him to read *The Lost World*) – but it is only apparently so, since he must assess whether his existence as a reader represents a debt that is to be paid or, on the contrary, an imposition for which he requires compensation. *Caveat lector*: he is placed in the position of the individual who must enter into a deal knowing that only retrospectively may it prove to have been well advised, but who at the same time must proceed in this manner if he is to attain the status of dealer and be incorporated into the systems of exchange prevailing in the community. This is the crux of the matter for the modern reader of Conan Doyle who may feel that he is purchasing aesthetic pleasure at the price of ideological compromise, a compromise which, because it acknowledges his cultural descent from the lost world of Doyle, minimises his chances of detaching himself from it.

As reader, I speak of myself as 'he' in the paragraph above, because it is explicitly a male community into which I am invited – author, characters, generic readership. At first sight, its status is pubertal, ontogenetically speaking, inasmuch as each reading member would seem to occupy a developmental position some-where between boy and man. But this is no doubt to read the epigraph too quickly. Who am I that I should read this story? Not at all a biological metamorph held in a state between puerility and virility. I am not *neither* but *both*, not lacking in specification but saturated with the ambivalence that is inscribed in the syntactic ambiguity of the 'who's. I am a boy 'who's' half a man in the sense that not all of the constituent characteristics of the adult man remain to be acquired: my aspiration to manhood is already an index of its potential realisation. I am also, however, a mature male 'who's' capable of a present regression to the apparently past moment when my manhood was still in question. In other words, I am engaged in the versatility of the verb *to be*, which designates that which I am, that which I might yet be, that which I might have been then, and that which I might have been now had my possibility of being been then other than it was. As for my future, it is prescribed by the text 'one hour of joy' – ample reason, one would think, to celebrate the finding of *The Lost World* and to acknowledge with a certain ambivalence the paternity of Conan Doyle.

In one respect, this text may be said to supply a missing link. The reader, called by both author and narrator to mediate between them, is, moreover, mediated by them, in the sense that he is

offered definitions of maturation and a fund of possible identifications in which his own maturation, anticipated or relived, may be
endorsed. It is this that makes of the critical reader an explorer and
requires him to say whether he likes what he finds. Pithecanthropic itself, it is appropriate that the novel should be concerned
with evolution. For its readership, it is deemed to constitute the
boundary between two ontogenetic sub-categories, boys and men,
each permeable by the other in an effort of imagination, and it
constitutes now a link between the ideological world of 1912 and
that, or those, of the 1980s. At the level of the narration the same
model obtains, as the cub reporter negotiates his rites of passage.
At the level of the narrated, the prehistoric is allowed to coexist
with the contemporary precisely in order that an imagined
synchrony may yield a dynamic male diachrony.

It is this prehistory that is unmentioned in the Sherlock Holmes
stories. Catherine Belsey has demonstrated the extent to which in
them female sexuality is rendered invisible and voiceless. What is
lacking is the Doylean account of origins, which in *The Lost World*
goes a long way towards explicating the genesis of this absence.
Holmes could emulate Cuvier in his reconstruction of extinct
entities and of past events, but he could not, like Professor
Challenger, encounter them in the flesh. There is none the less real
ideological continuity between the two detectors. Challenger's way
with women is quite consistent with the androcratic regime of
Baker Street. What is striking, however, is that his petite wife,
although physically manipulable, is at least allowed authoritative
utterances. 'He is a perfectly impossible person', she declares, and
her judgement is lifted from the flow of the fabula and established
as a chapter title by the judicious Mr Ed.

On close inspection, this particular narratorial device shows
indeed that in *The Lost World* the female deploys a diegetic force as
well as being an object of representation. The chapter titles operate
as trailers in that they hark forward to the chapter contents by
means of direction quotation. A survey of them reveals two
interesting features: first, those in which the narrator, Mr Ed.,
quotes himself cluster in the second half of the text and mark his
increasing maturity and ability to speak for himself; secondly, only
two of the titular utterances (two out of sixteen) emanate from
females and both are assigned to the early chapters in which the
two major characters are introduced (Mr Ed. in chapter 1, Professor
Challenger in chapter 3). These are not therefore silent females:

indeed, they are required to verbalise, for their annunciatory function confirms them as logical preconditions of the males. This is more clearly true of the female who impels Mr Ed. into narratorial activity, and what is interesting is that her sexuality is as yet unsilenced.

Sexual desire is the force that sets the text in motion. The young narrator is in love with Gladys, Gladys of the raven hair. Unhappily for him, he is maintained by her in a state of animated and non-virilised suspension. Aloof, withholding her sexuality, she acts as a barrier to that 'race-memory which we call instinct' and will not requite his love until he has achieved a manhood consistent with her own definition: 'There are heroisms all round us waiting to be done. It's for men to do them, and for women to reserve their love as a reward for such men.' This is how the call of the wild comes to Mr Ed. from a South London suburb. Tiring of fraternal companionship and longing to exchange the role of sibling for that of lover, he is, perfectly naturally, in the view of Gladys, packed off into nature in order to cure him of nature ('the primitive and the bestial'), or at least, and this is a different proposition, to render him eligible of it. For there is a paradox here, the resolution of which will seal the fate of the female and her role in the Doylean account of origins. It is in order that his nature may be naturalised that Mr Ed. is consigned to the wilderness, and in order that Gladys, for her part, might legitimately acknowledge him as natural when he returns – and reward him accordingly.

Gladys is not at all the attractive prude from whom the frustrated male turns in search of exotica. She has, in Mr Ed.'s curious phrase, 'all the stigmata of passion' and these endow her with considerable semiological power. Anatomically, her fertility is not in doubt, for the stigma, in the words of the *OED*, is 'the part of an ovisac where it ruptures to discharge the ovum'; psychologically, she carries the marks of the nineteenth-century hysteric, symbolising, if not somatising, an inability to assume her sexuality on any terms other than those of the androcratic order; morally, she becomes an object of reprobation and resentment which increase in proportion to desire; cosmologically, she acquires, by displacement no doubt from the narrator, a Christ-like capacity to suffer and to testify to suffering. A complex woman, then, with whom Mr Ed. has to deal at the level of the narrated. At the level of the narration, meanwhile, it is out her fertile complexity that the text is born.

The two levels are well co-ordinated. Once Gladys's annunciatory force is recognised then she cannot, narratologically speaking, go wrong. She is perfectly right to anticipate Mr Ed.'s early proposal of marriage and to deflect it in a manner which is ideologically so powerful. 'I should have done with suspense', he says, but she knows better. No suspense, no story; no suspense, no maturation; no suspense, no evolution; no suspense, no lost world found. Fortunately for Conan Doyle's (male) reader, Gladys is well informed as to her status as pretext. Were she not, then young Ned (for this is how she addresses her suitor) would never grow into Mr Ed. The metamorphosis, incidentally, is an interesting textual process incorporating acquisition of title (Mr), loss of initial upper-case N and acquisition of the full-stop of distinction. Sure enough, it is a fully fledged editorial figure that emerges in and from the wilderness, a narratorial agency capable of eliminating the negative, assigning titles, abbreviating where desirable and assuming full enunciatory authority.

One cannot feel that all this bodes well for Gladys. The problem, as posed at the outset, is that the cub reporter has to make a name for himself if he is to merit the 'one hour of joy' with her on his return. But has not this very hour already been promised by Conan Doyle to his male readership? Gladys is more or less forgotten once the party have left Southampton. It is true that her name is temporarily given to the primaeval lake, but this baptism of the baptismal waters merely confirms the logic of the fiction: namely, that the male is forged in his detachment from the female. In any case, once Mr Ed., having departed his native shores unnaturally, because prematurely, returns as a mature narrator, he finds that in the interim Gladys has married a solicitor's clerk. With all the newly acquired professional expertise at his disposal, he then undertakes the supreme editorial task, the abbreviation of his desire. It is at this point that the sexuality of Gladys is silenced, but it has by now served its purpose – that of giving life to the force capable of silencing it.

Initially Mr Ed. was dispatched by Gladys with instructions to emulate Henry Morton Stanley and Richard Burton. Burton, explorer and diplomat, has a certain semiological value in *The Lost World* because the majority of his notebooks were destroyed by his widow. It may be, then, that, in order to avoid elimination of the text by the female, the text makes a pre-emptive strike and eliminates the female. Lake Gladys is thus renamed Central Lake and the solicitor's clerk ensures that her sexuality, whatever potential she had for transcending cultural determinations, is absorbed into suburban routine.

The fate of the female in *The Lost World* adds an apparently diachronic dimension to the situation obtaining in the Holmes stories and described by Catherine Belsey. It seems clear that the female is present in the past in order to be able to initiate a course of events leading to a present from which it is desirable that she be absent. But why should this be? She presumably has a creative power which the male, as author, seeks to monopolise. Moreover, she giveth and she taketh away. She has a castrating potential that Mr Ed. realises symptomatically when he ventures into the primaeval garden armed, or disarmed, with a rifle and shot-gun pellets. She thus materially threatens the position and perceptions of the authorial agency, whose prerogative is to give and not to be taken away by a female. The Conan Doyle narrative system depends on female origins and male destinies and the hero is he who can effectively repudiate his origins in the female *fiat* and who can do so sufficiently successfully to impose silence on her and to exclude her from the world of discourse. Hence the brown hand that reaches across the table in the final sentence in a gesture of male solidarity. In this myth, the Amazons are men.

All this monosexuality really raises the question of the extent to which perceptions of alterity are indeed controlled. If the male is that which, having originated in the female, consolidates itself by a process of repudiation, is this ontogenesis repeated in the account of phylogenesis offered by the Doylean imagination? How does this masculine humanity stand in relation to the animal world? What type of evolutionism can be consistent with androcracy? It is interesting that the boundaries between the species are much less clear-cut than the boundary between the human sexes. The simple ambivalence, so to speak, displayed towards Gladys is narratologically less complex than the relations sustained with a great variety of fauna. Gladys's raven hair is but a weak specification when compared to the veritable bestiary of male characters who inhabit the text: Gladys's father, 'an untidy cockatoo'; McArdle, the crab-like editor of the *Daily Gazette*; fellow journalist Tarp Henry, a 'thin, dry, leathery creature'; the medical students, who are portrayed as carnivorous puppies; Professor Ronald Murray, who resembles a sheep; Professor Summerlee and his goat's beard; the equine Zambo, the faithful negro; the perfidious half-castes Gomes and Manuel, who are described as panthers; Mrs Challenger, both

canary and chicken; and, finally, Professor Challenger, so monstr-
ously polyvalent in this respect that he requires detailed scrutiny –
suffice it to say at the moment that even early in the text he is
presented as both bull and bull-frog and is given to hurling his
favourite insult, *porcus ex grege diaboli*, at tellers of tall tales such as
journalists and rival theoreticians of evolution.

The journalist Ed. Malone has been discussed above: it is his
origins that are implicitly theorised by the narration. The rival
evolutionist is interesting in a slightly different respect. Professor
Challenger, physical anthropologist and zoologist, is bitterly opposed to the theories of the German biologist August Weissmann.
Weissmann was as real and as historical a figure as Darwin, as well
as being as Darwinian as Challenger. On the other hand, he was
hostile to Lamarck's hypothesis of the genetic transmission of
acquired characteristics. He preferred his own notion of 'germ
plasm', a substance with a permanent structure, passed on in
reproduction and containing the essence of the species concerned –
an early prototype of DNA, in fact. He was also fiercely chauvinis-
tic and this did not endear him to the English imagination of 1912
which produced *The Lost World*. Challenger gives him short shrift:
'I protest strongly against the insufferable and entirely dogmatic
assertion that each separate *id* is a microcosm possessed of an
historical architecture elaborated slowly through the series of
generations.'

But what 'id' is this in an English text of 1912? Professor
Challenger owes his ultimate scientific achievement to a geological
accident, so the modern reader can hardly fail to dwell on a
terminological anomaly of such suggestiveness. Gladys, after all,
had imposed conditions on the id of Ned: thus it was that he
travelled in search of abbreviation, repudiated his origins and
became 'Ed.' Weissmann's piece of theoretical apparatus, however, has here lost its abbreviation. It should in fact be rendered
'id.', for 'idioplasm', the genetically significant protoplasm described above. There is, of course, no theoretical connection with
the Freudian id, which was born of Groddeck's *es* in 1923 and
which entered English in Latin, so to speak, in order to accompany
the psychologically well-established ego. The id., then, and the id
are unrelated and indeed incompatible, for, curiously enough, it
was in *Beyond the Pleasure Principle* that Freud contemplated turning
to Weissmann's biology for help in theorising the death instinct. It
remains fortuitously the case that Professor Challenger, challeng-

ing the id., becomes a proponent of the id, since, if by this syllable is designated a fund of instinctual energy, partly innate, partly acquired and repressed, then this may well be what he discovers in the lost world. The elite of the European and post-Columbian bestiary exhibited by the text becomes quite suddenly, at the scene of the geological accident, the human observer of Jurassic pterodactyls, dinosaurs, iguanodons and a whole host of repulsive entities that stretch the taxonomies of Western science.

This disconcerting discovery has powerful therapeutic implications, certainly as far as the narrator and his struggle for maturity are concerned. It also proves the existence of a contemporary prehistory, an existence which Challenger has long suspected and desired and which has aroused the resistance of all his professional colleagues as well as the lay public. That evolutionary laws might be suspended, that the past might persist, that regression might be possible, all this is deemed to be unthinkable by all but intellectual conquistadores of the calibre of Oedipus and Freud. 'Every great discoverer has been met with the same incredulity', says Challenger, 'Galileo, Darwin and I....' His motto is *vestigia nulla retrorsum*, 'never look rearwards', and does not mean that he counsels no truck with the past; instead, he denounces all representation of human temporality as a simple and mechanical linear sequence. For Challenger as for Freud, to bring the past into contact with the present is necessarily to construct the possibility of a different future. The biologistic Weissmann is attacked because evolution is not thought by Challenger to be reductive of consciousness.

My contention is that, if Challenger achieves the status of intellectual conquistador and if he escapes mechanical determinism, then he is necessarily something more than the ethnocentric explorer upholding the supposedly high standards of European civilisation in the heart of the darkness of South America. He is indeed far more complex and is not at all required by the text to purvey the stereotypical imperialism that might figure in the modern reader's expectations. True, there is the faithful black retainer and the villains are the half-castes; the Cucama Indians, however, are declared by Challenger to be 'an amiable but degraded race, with mental powers hardly superior to the average Londoner'. The mordant tones are not Lévi-Straussian, but the belief in the universal distribution of *pensée sauvage* certainly is.

Professor Challenger is, in fact, the paradigm of that which he discovers (shades of Freud once again) – namely, the coexistence of the prehistoric and the contemporary. For, while, unlike the iguanodons and the pterodactyls, whose bodies are too big for their brains, he and Professor Summerlee share the distinction of having brains too big for their bodies, this complementary excess places them in a status apart from that of the *fine fleur* of Western manhood and assigns Challenger, specifically, a position comparable in anomalousness to that of the king of the ape-men. So much does he resemble the missing link, the anthropoid ape (same torso, different cranium), that it is as if evolution has been suspended to a point at which the two can resume their life-histories in symbiosis.

In this curious way the text confounds both simple evolutionism and what Lévi-Strauss calls the false evolutionism of those (including Freud) who hold that the so-called primitive peoples embody the infancy of humanity. The Professor, despite being 'big and arresting and virile', with 'commanding gesture and masterful eyes', is, in the view of the narrator, childishly 'formidable and overbearing yet with a brain which has put him in the front rank of his scientific age'. Hence his predisposition in favour of the pterodactyl – 'the devil of our childhood in person'. Challenger, man and boy, embodies, at the level of the narrated, a sibling of the missing link and thus in a sense supplies a focus for the passing identification of the ideal pithecanthropic reader as he retraces his route to adulthood.

But, if it is Gladys's destiny to be a repudiated origin, it is Challenger's to be an abandoned mediation. Unhappily, the text does not succeed in living up to its intuitions. The narratorial ideology is far from enlightened and Mr Ed.'s rites of passage leave the Professor behind as the diachronic seeks to repress the synchronic. Prehistory becomes for the narrator and Lord John Roxton something out of which one must evolve and which must be left in the past only as the object of a dim and uncanny recollection. It is at this point that the male community constitutes itself, and at the level of the narrated it consists of Roxton and Mr Ed., together with the Indian inhabitants of the primaeval plateau, who, like the Europeans, have not actually evolved upon it.

Indian wisdom is said to designate the malevolence of the jungle as *curupuri*, the Tupi concept from which Brazilian Portuguese derives *curupurui*, the wren, *ave* (bird) *da familia dos trogloditidas*. And what is this if not the memory of chthonic origins, of birth from the soil? *Curupuri* is the wren, widely distributed throughout the American continent and known to Western ornithology as the cave-dweller because of its covered nest; it is the caves inhabited by the Indians, mode of ingress to and egress from the Jurassic plateau, and consequences of the volcanic activity which created it; it is Challenger himself, eccentric replica of the anthropoid ape and therefore mediator between *homo sapiens*, on the one hand, and *pan troglodytes*, *pan satyrus*, the chimpanzee, on the other. *Curupuri* is thus, among other things, Western academia with its two eminent representatives, Challenger and Summerlee, and its passionate wish to systematise the knowledge of its past.

The brown hand mentioned above, the one which motivates the final sentence of the novel, belongs to Lord John Roxton and is extended to Mr Ed. in the Albany as they project a return to the Jurassic plateau. They will go without Gladys, needless to say, but also without Challenger and Summerlee. It is noteworthy that Roxton, 'tall, thin', with 'humorous, masterful eyes', and Mr Ed. himself are the only two significant males who lack an animal coding. They do not belong, therefore, to the bestiary in which evidence of origins persists; they are the mature men who have had links with missing links which they intend to allow to go missing once more. These are the ideological heroes of the text and it is interesting to see what repudiations confer on them this status. The community to which they aspire to return is characterised as monosexual. It is not the prospect of a 'little red-skinned wife' that draws them back to the plateau; there will be no Gradiva through whom to regress, only a territory peopled by dwarfs who hope that no Snow White will ever reach them. It is as if the plateau, once insulated from the present, will in future be insulated from the past.

Roxton and Mr Ed. are not at all mythic heroes in the manner of Lévi-Strauss's Oedipus, seeking to reconcile beliefs in chthonic origins with the empirical knowledge of his gestation in Jocasta. In *The Lost World* the surviving heroes find another way of grappling with the two types of origins, the chthonic and the physiological, the evolutionary and the maternal, the phylogenetic and the ontogenetic: both are equally real and both are briefly acknowledged only to be ultimately repudiated. This, no doubt, is the price of the ideology of progress. It seems to me that heroism here consists in the ability to repress the desire for knowledge and, accordingly, the knowledge of desire. It consists in conforming to a male regime which systematically excludes three discrete categories of beings, without which it would never have achieved the power to exclude: ape-men, females and academics. Perhaps the modern reader, who may belong to one or more of these categories, is fortunate in that Conan Doyle was spectacularly sublimatory rather than repressive and much more imaginative than his sadly exemplary heroes. He or she is thus left with *The Lost World*, a symptom worthy of interpretation.

Notes

1. K. Chukovsky, *From Two to Five* (Berkeley, Calif.: University of California Press, 1966).
2. Arthur Conan Doyle, *The Lost World* (London: Hodder and Stoughton, 1912). All quotations from the novel are from this edition.
3. Catherine Belsey, *Critical Practice* (London: Methuen, 1981).
4. Sigmund Freud, quoted by Malcolm Bowie, 'Friend's Dreams of Knowledge', *Paragraph*, ii (1983) 53–87.

9

The House that Jack Built: Jack the Ripper, Legend and the Power of the Unknown

CLIVE BLOOM

Jack of Hearts, Jack O'Lantern, Jack the Giant-Killer, Jack the Lad – 'Jack' is a common name that represents ubiquity: the nomenclature of the ordinary. In the nineteenth century there was only one Jack – *the Ripper*; of the famous nineteenth-century criminals this one alone has endured into legend. Of Charlie Peace, Neill Cream or Israel Lipski little is remembered; of other famous murders only the victim is recalled: Maria Marten offering herself to melodrama and Fanny Adams to a coarse joke. Jack survives, but not merely because he was not caught.

This essay is an attempt to consider the determinants and the progress of the Ripper legend and to consider the constellation of historico-psychological notions that have gathered around the name of the Ripper.

Jack, it seems, timed his murders at a correct psychological moment, for almost immediately, not least for their ferocity, his deeds became the stuff of legend. He instantly became both a particular and a general threat, a focus for numerous related fears among metropolitan dwellers across Europe and America. One newspaper late in 1888 declared,

The Whitechapel murderer, having been arrested all over the metropolis and in several provincial towns, is now putting in an appearance in various foreign countries, and also in the United States of America . . . . [he is] a Russian with a religious mania . . . murdering Magdalens in order that their souls may go to heaven or [on New York advice] ... [He is] a butcher, whose mind is affected by changes of the moon.   (*The Times*, 3 Dec 1888)

Already, only one month after the murders had ceased, Jack has an international 'appeal'. His ubiquitous nature allows him appearances on both sides of the Atlantic and he is claimed by or accused of being a variety of nationalities. The article is already in light-hearted mood and Jack has taken on the serio-comic aspects of Sweeney Todd, himself a type of 'butcher'. Not only may he be both a Russian religious and sexual fanatic, but he may also be a New Yorker under biblical delusions (which the paper places under the 'Ezekiel Theory'). The Russian is not merely a religious fanatic but also a 'nihilist' and a member of a 'secret society' – Russia (the paper tells its readers) being notorious for secret societies. Thus, Jack becomes the focal point for an attack on foreigners (in particular Russians) and especially foreigners who are bent on undermining society in secret via covertly ritualised murder.

This mixture of grim charnel humour, political and religious fear, xenophobia and sexual innuendo (those journalistic 'Magdalens') partook of the atmosphere during the murders. At one end of the spectrum *Punch* (13 Oct 1888) dedicated a doggerel verse to the Ripper around a cartoon of Jack as a Mephistopheles bill-posting London with his latest exploits. This lampoon of the recent 'penny-dreadfuls' and 'Ripperana' was matched more seriously by the upsurge of anti-foreign agitation fanned by phantom messages (supposedly by the Ripper) accusing 'the Juwes', and by the Assistant Metropolitan Police Commissioner's claim that 'in stating that he [Jack] was a Polish Jew [he was] merely stating a definitely established fact' (which nearly started a pogrom in the East End).

On 13 February 1894 the *Sun*, a sensationalist newspaper, began printing a piece of popular investigative journalism about the 'real' Ripper, traced by 'WK', one of the staff reporters, to Broadmoor, 'a living tomb of a lunatic asylum' (17 Feb 1894) where the 'greatest murder mystery of the nineteenth century' was about to be solved by Jack the Ripper's 'confession'. This further accretion to the legend attempted to locate Jack in the world of 'debased' humanity in Broadmoor where inmates (and especially Jack) showed no moral awareness of the import of their deeds. In linking his home life to 'Camden Town' and his criminal insanity to Broadmoor the paper ably accused middle-class prudery of responsibility for Jack's upbringing. Nevertheless, the paper absolved that same class from blame by accepting that, in contrast to Jack, the paper's readers obviously possessed moral awareness. Curiosity was thus legitimised by a veneer of morality.

Unlike the clippings of the 1880s, this series put together insanity and the middle class. The murders were already thought of as the work of a depraved doctor. Nevertheless, the linking of 'the greatest murder mystery' and a 'living tomb' put together mysteriousness and living death in a way guaranteed *not* to reveal the killer's identity and guaranteed to increase sales of the *Sun* for the duration of the series. Moreover, the paper could congratulate itself and its readers on tracking down the perpetrator without undoing the 'edge' of fear they wished to create – for, as the paper clearly stated, this lunatic had *escaped* in order to kill. So horrible was he, so morally unaware, that armed guards stood about his bed. Jack's ubiquity is therefore reinforced by his unnamed status (he is identified only by initials) and by the hints of his origins and his ability to vanish from the lunatic asylum at will if not guarded. The lunatic asylum was represented by the paper as a type of purgatorial doom from which the 'living dead' returned to reap vengeance on the twilight world of the living (twilight, precisely because the victims were prostitutes). One mysterious world preys on another. Indeed, by returning from Broadmoor the journalist literally returns from the dead to tell his tale.

Medical and criminological science are used in this series to reinforce secrecy and threat; commercialism dictates the possibility of other (and) endless articles on the Ripper.

However, even during the season of the killings in the autumn of 1888, papers quickly realised the value of Jack's exploits, conducting their own post-mortems and reporting coroners' verdicts at length. *The Times*, for instance, ran articles in its *Weekly Edition* from September 1888 to November 1888. On 28 September 1888 it gave a full page to the social background of Spitalfields and the poverty endured there by Annie Chapman, the Ripper's first victim. *The Times* was quick to guess the direction in which police might look. They thought a post-mortem surgeon's assistant might be the culprit because of 'his' specialised knowledge of the uterus, which was removed from the victim's body.

The Times further noted the curious circumstance of an American surgeon who wished to include real uteri with a journal he was mailing to clients! Could this bizarre surgeon, whose name was not known, have prompted the killer to get 'a uterus for the £20 reward?' asked the paper. In a later issue, next to the report of other Ripper murders (26 Oct 1888), a clergyman protested in a long letter at the condemnation of the destitute by the middle classes, at their hypocrisy over prostitution and at their ignorance of the conditions prevailing in the East End. He concluded that this had 'blotted the pages of our Christianity'.

The freakish, of which the nineteenth century was inordinately fond, found itself beside the missionary, which in its guise as Mayhew, Engels or Booth consistently restated the ordinariness of the 'freak' (the destitute, the prostitute, the opium addict, the derelict). 'Body snatching' (and the notion of a uterus as a 'free gift' with a new journal) then weirdly allies itself with murder for greed (the reward offered of £20) and murder as the act of the desperately destitute. Jack becomes the focus for the bizarre in the ordinary misery of everyday life in the metropolitan slums. Jack the murderer becomes Jack *the missionary* who focused on problems other investigators were unable to bring to such a wide audience. Murder allowed for social reform. The newspapers, by keeping Jack the centre of attention, ironically kept the slum problems central too.

After reports covering three months by *The Times* and *The Times Weekly Edition*, the newspaper concluded that 'the murderer seems to have vanished, leaving no trace of his identity ... with even greater mystery' (*The Times*, 10 Nov 1888). Jack the Ripper, given his *nom de guerre* by Fleet Street, was the first major figure to offer himself to, and to become, a creation of journalism. By the 1880s newspapers commanded audiences large enough to make Jack a major figure of international interest rather than a local folktale figure for the East End of London.[1] The power of journalism and the crowded warrens of the central city of the Empire together provided ground for the dissemination of the legend, a legend based upon both fear *and* curiosity – a terrible ambivalence. The possibilities for the dissemination of *rumour* could never be more fortuitous, and letters from 'Jack' fed interest and added to the atmosphere of uncertainty.

Indeed, Jack's letters themselves may have been the work of an entrepreneurial journalist providing 'copy' for himself. These letters, conveying a black humour and a certain 'bravado' (*Stratford Express*, 7 May 1965), may be read not merely as the realisation of the power (for the first time) of the mass media but, whether authentic or fake, yet another accretion to the fictionalising of the Ripper and the self-advertising and self-confidence of an entrepreneurial murderer (acquiring kudos by self-advertisement).

These letters convey a music-hall atmosphere and a self-important theatricality through which the Ripper's letters create an imaginary persona for the perpetrator. Addressed to 'the Old Boss', and signed (at least once) 'from Hell', Jack goes into his music-hall act for the bewildered audience – appalled, amazed (and applauding) the virtuoso performance. 'He' tells us that

> I was goin' to hopperate again close to your ospitle – just as i was goin to drop my nife along at er bloomin throte them curses of coppers spoilt the game but i guess i will be on the job soon and will send you another bitt of innerd.

In another letter he finds the search for his identity a source of amusement: 'They say I am a doctor now. Ha! Ha!'

Each letter becomes a performance put on by an actor assuming a part. The letter-writing gives a self-importance to the writer and a grandeur and status which is uncompromised by capture and identification. Hence, this letter activity becomes, for the legend at least, as important as the deeds themselves; as Davy Crockett or P. T. Barnum were to make legends of their own lives by writing their autobiographies and adventures. The Ripper letters are a form of *true life confession* heightened to the level of a fiction which embraces a 'cockney' persona, a sense of black humour, a melodramatic villain ('them curses of coppers') and a ghoul (sending 'innerds'), and mixes it with a sense of the dramatic and a feeling for a rhetorical climax. In these letters life and popular theatre come together to act upon the popular imagination. The Ripper (now possibly many 'Rippers' all reporting their acts) autographs his work as a famous artist (death as creativity) – anonymous and yet totally well known. Here, confession only adds to confusion (even Neill Cream claimed to be the Ripper). Jack's letter 'from Hell' concludes 'catch me when you can', adding a sense of challenge and a stronger sense of a 'hint' to the frustration of authority in its quest for an actual identity to the murderer.[2] By the time of these letters Jack has ceased to be one killer but has become a multiplicity of performing personas for the imagination. The possibility of copycat crimes (although finally dismissed from at least two other 'torso' cases) lent to Jack the amorphous ability to inhabit more than one physical body (a point which I shall develop later).

Consequently, for the late nineteenth century, the Ripper became a type of 'folk' character whose exploits spilled into the twentieth century via cinema, theatre and fiction. In our own century the Ripper has been tracked and traced by numerous writers after a positive identity. Writers have named a Russian doctor called Konovalov (Donald McCormick), the Duke of Clarence (Thomas Stowell), William Gull (Stephen Knight), Montague Druitt (Daniel Farson) and J. K. Stephen (Michael Harrison) as possible candidates. Each, in his turn, has been refuted – the 'royal theory' being denied by Walter Sickert's son Joseph, who dismissed it as a hoax that he had played on an over-receptive author. The 'debate' heats up every few years with new flushes of theory and further refutations, while works such as Knight's *Jack the Ripper: The Final Solution* add to the growing heap of books searching for scandal in suburbia or in the freemasons, in highest government or the royal family.[3] Knight, himself a journalist, stated in the *East London Advertiser* (7 Dec 1973) that 'the evil presence of Jack the Ripper still seems to haunt . . . the imagination of crime investigators', and he notes that in the 1970s letters were still arriving from people claiming knowledge of or claiming actually to be 'the Ripper'. In the twentieth century Jack has become the centre of a conspiracy debate. Indeed, so vast is the volume of literature to date that Alexander Kelly was able to write an article for *The Assistant Librarian* about his compilation of a bibliography of 'Ripperana and Ripperature'.[4] As Geoffrey Fletcher in the *Daily Telegraph* (9 Oct 1974) commented, 'hence it is that Jack belongs not only to the criminologist, but also to folklore'.

The first part of this essay dealt with the rapid dissemination of the Ripper legend and its endurance in popular publishing. I now wish to turn to the constellation of possibilities around which this publishing industry revolved and upon which the legend was built.

It is obvious that any legend requires a small and possibly spectacular fact to unleash a great deal of 'fiction'. Before turning to the legend as a type of 'fictional' genre it is necessary to consider the Ripper legend as revolving around (a) a series of bizarre and ferocious crimes, (b) an impotent and mocked authority (the

Criminal Investigation Department being left totally in the dark and being criticised from Windsor[5]), (c) a mysterious and unapprehended felon, and (d) the power of fiction and the use of the human sciences.

The murders of autumn 1888 allowed for the appearance of a new urban dweller, a dweller on the limits of society and yet fully integrated into it – the homicidal maniac, *the psychopathic killer*. Unlike de Sade, the psychopath is always *in disguise*; his intentions and his secret actions are on another plain from his social responsibilities. Consequently, the psychopath delineates that absolute psychological and mental 'deterioration' that Kraepelin had considered as a form of dementia praecox and that was not defined as schizophrenia until 1911. The Ripper, however, was seen as split not merely in personality but in *morality* as well. The case of the psychopath is a case not of deterioration of mental power but of a demonic engulfing of the egotistic soul by a monstrous and sensuous will. Here the psychopath unites theology and science, unites the lowest and the highest impulses in his society. The psychopath is ill and yet suffers only from an overwhelming need to impose his will on his surroundings. The psychopath 'lets go' only in order to secrete his lost personality more fully in those daylight hours of responsibility. The demonic had not yet lost its force in the 1880s, reinforced as it was by scientific research.

In order to explore the paradox of the psychopath more fully we can turn to the popular fiction of the 1880s. Robert Louis Stevenson's *Dr Jekyll and Mr Hyde* was published in 1886, two years before 'Jack' made his own spectacular appearance.[6]

Stevenson's story deals specifically with split personality – split between the sensual and the socially and morally responsible. Jekyll is the epitome of middle-class propriety, living in a street described as having houses with 'freshly painted shutters well polished brasses and general cleanliness' (p. 30), while Hyde is a monstrous and 'ape-like' (p. 47) maniac who lives amid the sexual depravity of Soho: 'that dismal quarter of Soho seen under these changing glimpses, with its muddy ways, and slatternly passengers, and its lamps, which had never been extinguished or had been kindled afresh to combat this mournful reinvasion of darkness, seemed, in the lawyer's eyes, like a district of some city in a nightmare' (p. 48).

This duality of personality and class (the more working-class the more depraved) is considerably complicated by Stevenson's own mixing of Darwinism and pseudo-science. Degeneracy for Stevenson (as for Edgar Allan Poe in 'The Murders in the Rue Morgue') is a decline in to an animal state – the noble savage has become the sex-crazed ape. However, this motif (repeated by Rider Haggard in *She*) is interrupted by a 'psychological' study of Jekyll from whose dark side Hyde is generated. Jekyll has always been aware of his dual nature:

> Hence it came about that I concealed my pleasures; and ... I stood already committed to a profound duplicity of life ... that made me what I was and, with even a deeper trench than in the majority of men, severed in me those provinces of good and ill which divide and compound man's dual nature. In this case, I was driven to reflect deeply and inveterately on that hard law of life which lies at the root of religion, and is one of the most plentiful springs of distress. Though so profound a double-dealer, I was in no sense a hypocrite; both sides of me were in dead earnest; I was no more myself when I laid aside restraint and plunged in shame, than when I laboured, in the eye of day, at the furtherance of knowledge or the relief of sorrow and suffering. And it chanced that the direction of my scientific studies ... led wholly towards the mystic and the transcendental. (p. 81)

Indeed, it is Jekyll's very aspirations toward the ideal that have caused his degeneracy. Such a duality makes Jekyll tell his friend that 'if [he is] the chief of sinners [he is] the chief of sufferers too' (p. 58).

Highlighted here is not schizophrenia as illness but Jekyll's schizoid nature as showing signs of *moral* degeneracy. Mental decay is seen as a consequence of original sin lurking in the hearts of all men of whatever class – the more denied (by the respectable) the more virulent its final outburst. Stevenson makes this quite plain in his description of Hyde's manic progress during the opening narrative. He lets his narrator tell us that 'then came the horrible part of the thing; for the man trampled calmly over the child's body and left her screaming on the ground. It sounds nothing to hear, but it was hellish to see. It wasn't like a man; it was like some damned Juggernaut' (p. 31).

Hyde becomes an abominable *it*, a desecration of the sanity of the human causing revulsion even in the doctor who witnesses the deed (p. 31). Equally this combines with fear at the bizarre and freakish appearance of the culprit: 'There is something wrong with his appearance; something displeasing, something downright detestable. I never saw [a man] I so disliked, and yet I scarce know why. He must be deformed somewhere; he gives a strong feeling of deformity' (p. 34). Hyde combines animality and the terror of the 'troglodytic' (p. 40) with fear of evil, for he has 'a kind of black sneering coolness . . . really like Satan' (p. 32).

This mixture of the animal and the devilish comes from the perverse idealism of Jekyll, a scientist and pillar of society who is bent on unlocking *his own* potential for experiencing the limits of perception through the power of his own will. His science is therefore put to the cause of metaphysical speculation. He tells us that, 'it chanced that the direction of his scientific studies . . . led wholly toward the mystic and transcendental' (p. 81). Here, then, the scientist manipulates the soul in order to reorganise the nature of the body, for, in destroying the 'fortress of identity' Jekyll employs science as if it were magic (p. 83); 'man is not truly one, but truly two' (p. 82).

Stevenson's short story became a massive popular hit when published. In it he summed up the pseudo-science of the popular imagination as well as the confused state of the emergent psychological sciences which were 'treating' schizophrenic patients. The psychopath (Mr Hyde is such through his maniacal killing for killing's sake and the enjoyment he gains) crosses the border of scientific discourse and acts as its limit, beyond the rational explanations of form and natural function. Instead, the psychopath takes us beyond science and before it into theology, into the analysis of *sin*.

In picking upon this duality Stevenson made repeated statements about the nature of evil and its relationship with insanity. He tells us,

The pleasures which I made haste to seek in my disguise were, as I have said, undignified; I would scarce use a harder term. But in the hands of Edward Hyde they soon began to turn towards the monstrous. When I would come back from these excursions, I was often plunged into a kind of wonder at my vicarious depravity. This familiar that I called out of my own soul, and sent forth alone to do his good pleasure, was a being inherently malign and villainous; his every act and thought centred on self.... The situation was apart from ordinary laws, and insidiously relaxed the grasp of conscience. It was Hyde, after all, and Hyde alone, that was guilty. Jekyll was no worse; he woke again to his good qualities seemingly unimpaired; he would even make haste, where it was possible, to undo the evil done by Hyde. And thus his conscience slumbered.

(pp. 86–7)

Here the 'monstrous' connects with meta-laws that organise consciousness but cannot escape from it, for *will* (according to Jekyll's philosophy) and the drive to power dominate the consciousness of mankind. According to Stevenson, from the socially responsible, the morally restrained and the intellectually ideal come anarchy, moral degeneracy and perversity dominated by a Calvinistic notion of predestined sin.

As with Jekyll and Hyde so Jack the Ripper was seen as an inhuman if not non-human monster who combined possible middle-class respectability (a doctor or a surgeon) with lower-working-class savagery (an immigrant, 'Leather-Apron', a mad butcher). The Ripper united both classes inasmuch as he was excluded by his acts from both (just as were his victims). The Ripper was both a technician (a post-mortem surgeon, a doctor, a butcher) and an insane lunatic (incapable of finesse). He was supposedly at once able to focus his aggression in anatomical detail and yet unable to curb its force. Thus, the forensic nature of the Ripper's 'work' (his 'job') provided a focal point for popular fears and prejudices against those professions dealing in the limits of the 'decent' (psychologists, doctors, post-mortem surgeons, forensic experts). The Ripper's supposed anatomical expertise suggested all sorts of horrible possibilities about the life of the 'expert' and the specialist. His ability with a knife united him to the very professionals paid to track him down!

Like Hyde, he was the *alter ego* of the police force and the letters clearly demonstrate him showing off his expertise to them and the vigilante forces operating in Whitechapel. Later his dual nature as criminal and enforcer-of-law became explicit when reports of his deerstalker gave one attribute to the occupier of 221b Baker Street, whose business was forensic science, whose other real-life model was a surgeon and whose friend was a doctor.

Thus the Ripper was not merely a murderer but the catalyst for a series of psychological and social reactions. He combined the supposed popular idea of the expert as well as the darker side of the madman, lunatic, animal degenerate. As a median point between middle-class respectability and a debased Darwinian proletariat, the Ripper became the invisible man; like Jekyll he might well have said that 'for him in his impenetrable mantle, the safety was complete. Think of it – he did not exist!' (p. 86). The Ripper's letters acknowledge the pretence of cockney patois while pointing directly toward a middle-class author – but the author of what: a letter or the murders? The Ripper is both murderer and social 'reformer', both scientist and magician.

In the previous section of this essay we have seen that the combination of popular prejudice and fiction produced a character and a rationale for the Ripper *qua* murderer *and* respectable member of society. His split nature (if such it was or presumably had to be) was completed by a hypocrisy concerning the very people he killed (the 'Magdalens'). For these people were themselves invisible, acting as a certain outlet *and* limit to urban society. The psychopath and the prostitute were two ends of a society that refused to acknowledge their presence. Invisibly, they provided their services on the edge of the rational, morally degenerate as both supposedly were.

Yet Jack the Ripper's threat is one that spills back into 'ordinary' society and threatens that society. In the period when the legend of 'the Ripper' begins, the psychopath becomes an urban reality but as a character-type is not quite part of a mental spectrum and yet is not fully freed from being a theological problem either. Jack combines notions of evil, insanity and moral justice at the moment when the nineteenth century saw itself as the century of progress, enlightenment and escape from 'moral' prejudice. The Ripper's name denotes a certain consequent frontier for the human sciences at this time.

At the culminating point of the human sciences came the science of legitimised 'murder'. James Berry, the public executioner at the time of the 'Ripper' murders, wrote his autobiography in the 1890s and in it we see combined Jack's role as breaker *and* upholder of the law and of natural justice.[7] Berry, who became an abolitionist (he decapitated one of his clients because of an incorrect 'drop'), viewed his work as 'a job like any other'[8] and H. Snowden Ward in his appraisal called Berry 'tender-hearted'.[9] This business-like and tender-hearted man carried out public executions and gave his rope to Madame Tussaud's. His contribution to the human sciences was to calculate the proportion of rope needed relative to body weight, in order to cause death without mutilation of the victim. He also endeavoured to 'understand' the mind of a murderer, whom, unlike the general public, he viewed as neither a 'fiend' nor a 'monster'.[10] He commented that he hoped he could 'advise his readers to consider that a murderer has as much right to judge the state as the state has to judge him',[11] which is an oddly radical comment for the ultimate enforcer of the state's law! Indeed, Berry saw quite clearly the anomaly of his position.[12] Hence he becomes both killer and killed, both culprit and re-venger, both state appointee and state victim. Within Berry's own person these ambiguities were traced.

James Berry and Jack the Ripper are joined by the technology of death. This unites and yet ultimately separates their purposes, for Berry participates in the oddly humanitarian enterprise that Michel Foucault sees as a movement from torture to the timetable in dealing with miscreants. Berry, working in secret, takes on the onus of the executioner's task as a duty as well as a job. His book portrays a deep ambivalence as well as pride in work well done. The business of death puts professionalism at a premium. Berry's expertise is, however, the expertise of an almost defunct crafts-man, for, although hanging remained for another eighty years, its power was severely limited and its function debilitated by secrecy and humanitarian concern. The acknowledged schizoid nature of the executioner begins to crack open in James Berry and his autobiography in his constant justifications and special pleading. The Ripper takes pride in his particular executions, for Jack belongs to another *older* tradition of execution.

Michel Foucault, quoting eighteenth-century sources, gives the grisly details of the form of public execution then required in France:

The executioner, who had an iron bludgeon of the kind used in slaughter houses, delivered a blow with all his might on the temple of the wretch, who fell dead: the *mortis exactor*, who had a large knife, then cut his throat, which spattered him with blood; it was horrible sight to see; he severed the sinews near the two heels, and then opened up the belly from which he drew the heart, liver, spleen and lungs, which he stuck on an iron hook, and cut and dissected into pieces, which he then stuck on the other hooks as he cut them, as one does with an animal.[13]

We may compare this to Jack's own 'private' (but very public) methods. His last victim, 'Mary Kelly ... was lying on her back on a bed, where she had been placed after the murderer cut her throat ... he set to work mutilating the body, which was stabbed, slashed, skinned, gutted and ripped apart. Her nose and breast were cut off; her entrails were extracted: some were removed.'[14]

In the eighteenth century executions became a ritual in which the 'main character was the people, whose ... presence was required for the performance'.[15] By Jack's time public execution was long since over, but Jack took on the symbolic weight of a 'higher' justice operating beyond the arm of the law, exposing and cutting out the cancer of sexual commerce. His role was acknowledged in his instant fame and his ferocity in his attack on the condemned: the prostitute class. It appears that Jack represented the return of a social memory of the proximity of death (by violence, cholera, starvation) now distanced by the work of social and medical reformers.

In that latter half of the industrialised nineteenth century ceremonies about the integration of death had long ceased to be necessary. In a sense the body had gained utility value but lost its 'sacred' humanness (its 'mystery' that early Christians feared). Jack represents the unconscious of that society – a repression not yet exorcised; he forcibly reminded society (unable to speak of bodies without blushing) of the crudest function of that mass of organs. Jack clearly unites ideas about the mortification of the flesh and the technology that manipulates the body (the human sciences: biology, psychology, forensic science, medicine). One end of the spectrum acknowledges desire for and the power of the flesh whilst the other denies both and reduces the body to a mass of functions and utilities: an automaton. The body hence becomes ironically 'sacred' (as an object in religious devotion to be escaped *from*) and yet also machinic.

Yet the savagery of Jack's attacks suggests more. As the attacks became more savage, so the mutilation of the victim became more complete. Finally it took pathologists six hours to piece together the empty shell of Mary Kelly scattered around the room in which she died. For Jack this final attack meant more than an attempt to punish womankind for its sins and its tempting flesh. Here the body is emptied, turned into a shell into which the murderer could plunge his knife and hands. The emptying assumes the form of an attempt to 'go beyond' the boundaries of flesh in a 'new' and horrific way. This violence demolishes and liquefies the body, which flows away and takes with it its ego boundaries. The body is opened, penetrated, dissected, made totally possessable.

As the bodily boundaries vanish we are reminded of the search for the auguries at Rome, a desperate search for a stable and knowable destiny. As the uterus determines the growing foetus, so the 'innerds' of the female body offer themselves for decoding. But what do they signify? Nothing, or more properly, an absence, *for the place of origin is missing*. The quest carried out by the probing knife reveals only a mess of tangled 'innerds'. Jack's attack signifies a *going beyond* toward an otherness that is totally non-human. The object and the possessor mesh into one critical quest.

What did Jack search for? Inside the body, finally opened, the culprit used the technique of a manic autopsy in order to find the non-body: the beyond and yet absolute of his own existence – his *soul* perhaps? In finding this origin Jack may have been able to find his own significance unhindered by the body which forced him to kill. For Jack as for his public, these killings, graphically illustrated and documented in the popular press, may have signified, as they still may do, the final frenzied acknowledgement of the coming of the age of materialism.

The body of 'the Magdalen' signifies the absence of purity and the presence of sin; but what does each weigh – what atomic weight can be assigned to the soul? Can the significance of the Ripper's violence, which has fascinated readers and researchers for so long, be explained in this way – that his quest was for a lost and discarded origin and that his method was a repressed and supposedly outdated one? The object of Jack's killing is not to take on the power of 'the other' but to *bypass 'the other' altogether* in order to confront *otherness* itself.

This may be borne out perhaps in the nature and morbid (perhaps healthy?) interest of generations of readers. Jack's killing partakes of a deep sub-stratum of cultural knowledge, a cultural awareness of the nature of sacrifice. If this appears far-fetched we can turn to René Girard's *Violence and the Sacred*, an anthropological work which appeared in 1972.[16]

First, though, let me briefly recapitulate the ideas outlined above. I have drawn attention to the dual nature of the popular notion of alienation – both demonic and machinic, with its consequent ambiguities over the relationship of victim to killer: social pillar and social pariah. At this juncture the psychotic killer, a product of urban life at the end of the nineteenth century, appears as both mentally defective and metaphysically gifted – both cancer and purgative. I have further suggested the possibilities and limits of Jack's 'quest' and the disturbance to identity that that caused. To further this inquiry let us now return to Girard's work on sacrifice.

Girard tells us that initially 'the sacrificial act assumes two opposing aspects, appearing at times a sacred obligation ... at others a sort of criminal activity'. He notes the 'ambivalent' nature of sacrifice but says this does not fully account for its 'value'.[17] In his view, 'sacrifice contains an element of mystery',[18] and it is this mystery that he wishes to penetrate. Quoting Joseph de Maistre, he adds, 'the sacrificial animals were always those most prized for their gentleness, most innocent creatures, whose habits ... brought them most closely into harmony with man'.[19] Indeed, we are told that 'sacrificial victims are almost always animals'.[20]

Here then we see that Jack the Ripper and James Berry share both a criminal and a 'sacred' (legitimised by the state) obligation. Berry acknowledged the ambivalence in his role. Moreover, in both cases, secrecy adds an air of mystery to the proceedings. The 'Magdalens' fit the role of sacrificial 'animals' through their own ambiguous position: both gentle, and aggressive in selling their wares; innocent and sexually aware; *and* in harmony with 'man' while in competition with and engaged in commercial transactions with him.

We may go further, for Girard points out that the very lowest (slaves) and the very highest (sacrificial kings) are the ends of the sacrifice spectrum.[21] But he concludes that 'in many cultures women are never, or rarely, selected as sacrificial victims',[22] because of the feuds this would cause between husbands and children and the class that claims them. However, these points can be easily met, for prostitutes are both 'animals' and 'Magdalens'; both subhuman and sacred. Moreover, in the culture of which we speak these women are precisely those that were forced (therefore to the popular mentality *chose*) to break all their ties with husbands, children, class. They became the sacrificial victims for that culture, without ties or kinsfolk to gain revenge on their behalf. At one end of our spectrum Jack does nothing illegitimate – *but* his act is illegal for he kills outside the *context* of the sacrificial system (long since forgotten, of course, in the nineteenth century). His act is both sacred and lunatic, bestial and totally 'sane'.

Moreover, Jack's acts of sacrifice/murder appeal to a deeply archaic level of human response – a response long since channelled elsewhere into 'humane' destruction for sane offenders and lunatic asylums for 'morally degenerate' offenders. In the 1880s these two conditions partook of a peculiar mixture of demonic ability and psychological disintegration neither properly disentangled from the other in either the popular imagination, literature or the human sciences.

Yet we must go deeper to fathom the legendary power of Jack (for structuralist approaches consider the action of legend and myth in too formalistic a way). We have seen the specific historico-psychological aspects of the Ripper's enduring fame. But we must return to Girard for our final formulation of his power over our imaginations.

Girard considers sacrifice an attempt by society to 'deflect upon a relatively indifferent victim ... the violence that would otherwise be vented on its own members, the people it most desires to protect'.[23] Consequently 'the sacrifice serves to protect the entire community from *its own violence*'.[24]

Let us return to *Dr Jekyll and Mr Hyde*. Jekyll *generates* from *his own* personality the characteristics of the psychopath. His dual nature partakes *not* of a ghostly *Doppelgänger* but of aspects from *within* himself. His violence is a hatred of his own class and its expectation of restraint and decorum – its understanding of order. Girard comments on the Bible story of Cain and Abel that 'Cain's "jealousy" of his brother is only another term for his own characteristic trait: his lack of sacrificial outlet'.[25] Right at the beginning of *Dr Jekyll and Mr Hyde* we are introduced to Mr Utterson the lawyer, the ultimate figure of respectability, who 'was austere with himself' and who says of himself, 'I incline to Cain's heresy' (p. 29). As with Jekyll, it is more than a psychological problem; it is 'deeper'. Like Jack, Jekyll crosses a profound border, a border that disturbed 'anthropologists' and theologians alike in the nineteenth century.[26]

Thus we see the truly ritualistic and 'psychological' nexus of Jack's violence, for his work dissolves boundaries, acts as a gaping maw into which perception of order and rightness are sucked.

Jack's *name* as well as his deeds and the *deeds in his name* disturb our order, trangress boundaries, translate legitimacy into illegitimacy and the sacred into the bestial *and translate them back again*. For Jack there is no 'other', only a gaping hole within self that is beyond reconciliation with laws of man or God.

Jack, like any legendary figure, represents this *effectively* because he steps out of historical circumstance and into the imagination of the future. As such, like King Arthur or Robin Hood or Count Dracula, he is the *undead*. Jack, however, bypasses the criminal *underworld*, for he does not belong to it. He is outside that underworld, which is itself defined within the comprehension of the living (the non-animal). Jack is demon/animal and therefore totally other, therefore unrecognisable (invisible), therefore the perfect criminal. He disturbs the human only to reinforce it. Indeed, this monstrosity embeds himself in the imagination of each generation that *needs* his presence. For that reason alone there is a smile on the face of the Ripper.

Notes

1.   'In appearance, a paper of the 1890s was a product substantially the same as our own ... the phrase "new journalism" was first used by the poet Matthew Arnold of the lively work of the *Pall Mall Gazette* and its competitors in the late 1880s. This was indeed the seedbed of the twentieth century commercial popular press. ... There was also a new group of evening papers circulating in London and going out aggressively for new readers. ... It was these evening papers which first educated the morning papers into editorial policies suitable for the masses. Kennedy Jones and Alfred Harnsworth (later Lord Northcliffe) worked out their ideas for mass journalism for there was a new generation emerging in the years after the Great Exhibition of 1851 which had great curiosity but little education' – Anthony Smith, *The Newspaper: An International History* (London: Thames and Hudson, 1979) pp. 153–4.

2.   Letters quoted by C. M. McCleod in *The Criminologist*, no. 9 (1968) 120–7.

3.   Stephen Knight, *Jack the Ripper: The Final Solution* (London: Grafton, 1976).

4.   Alexander Kelly, 'Ripperana and Ripperature', *The Assistant Librarian*, 1973, pp. 3–6.

5.   T. A. Critchley, *A History of Police in England and Wales* (London: Constable, 1978) p. 161.

6.   Robert Louis Stevenson, *Dr Jekyll and Mr Hyde*, in *Dr Jekyll and Mr Hyde and Other Stories*, ed. Jenni Calder (Harmondsworth: Penguin,

1983). All quotations from the story are from this edition. Page references are given in the text.

7. James Berry, *My Life as an Executioner*, ed. Jonathan Goodman (Newton Abbot: David and Charles, 1972).
8. Ibid., p. 1.
9. Ibid., p. 11.
10. Ibid., p. 66.
11. Ibid., p. 95.
12. Ibid.
13. Michel Foucault, *Discipline and Punish*, tr. Alan Sheridan (London: Allen Lane, 1977) p. 53.
14. Gordon Honeycomb, *The Murders of the Black Museum 1870–1970* (London: Hutchinson, 1982).
15. Foucault, *Discipline and Punish*, p. 57.
16. René Girand, *Violence and the Sacred*, tr. Patrick Gregory (Baltimore: Johns Hopkins University Press, 1977).
17. Ibid., p. 1.
18. Ibid.
19. Ibid., p. 2.
20. Ibid., p. 9.
21. Ibid., p. 12.
22. Ibid.
23. Ibid., p. 4.
24. Ibid., p. 8.
25. Ibid., p. 4.
26. René Girard, 'Myth and Ritual in Shakespeare: *A Midsummer Night's Dream*' in *Textual Strategies*, ed. Josué V. Harrari (London: Methuen, 1980) pp. 189–212.

Index